BeforeThey Were Giants

Portraits of African American Sheroes and Heroes

By Amari Rashad and Dr. AMN

This book belongs to:

SSG

Saleem Shakir Gilmore books may be purchased in bulk at special discounts for sales promotion, corporate gifts, fundraising, or educational purposes. Special editions can also be created to specifications. For details, contact Saleem Shakir Gilmore at saleemgilmore@gmail.com

Join our community at www.facebook.com/beforetheyweregiants

Print ISBN: 979-8-218-27427-6

Library of Congress Control Number: 2023917971

Printed in the U.S.A.

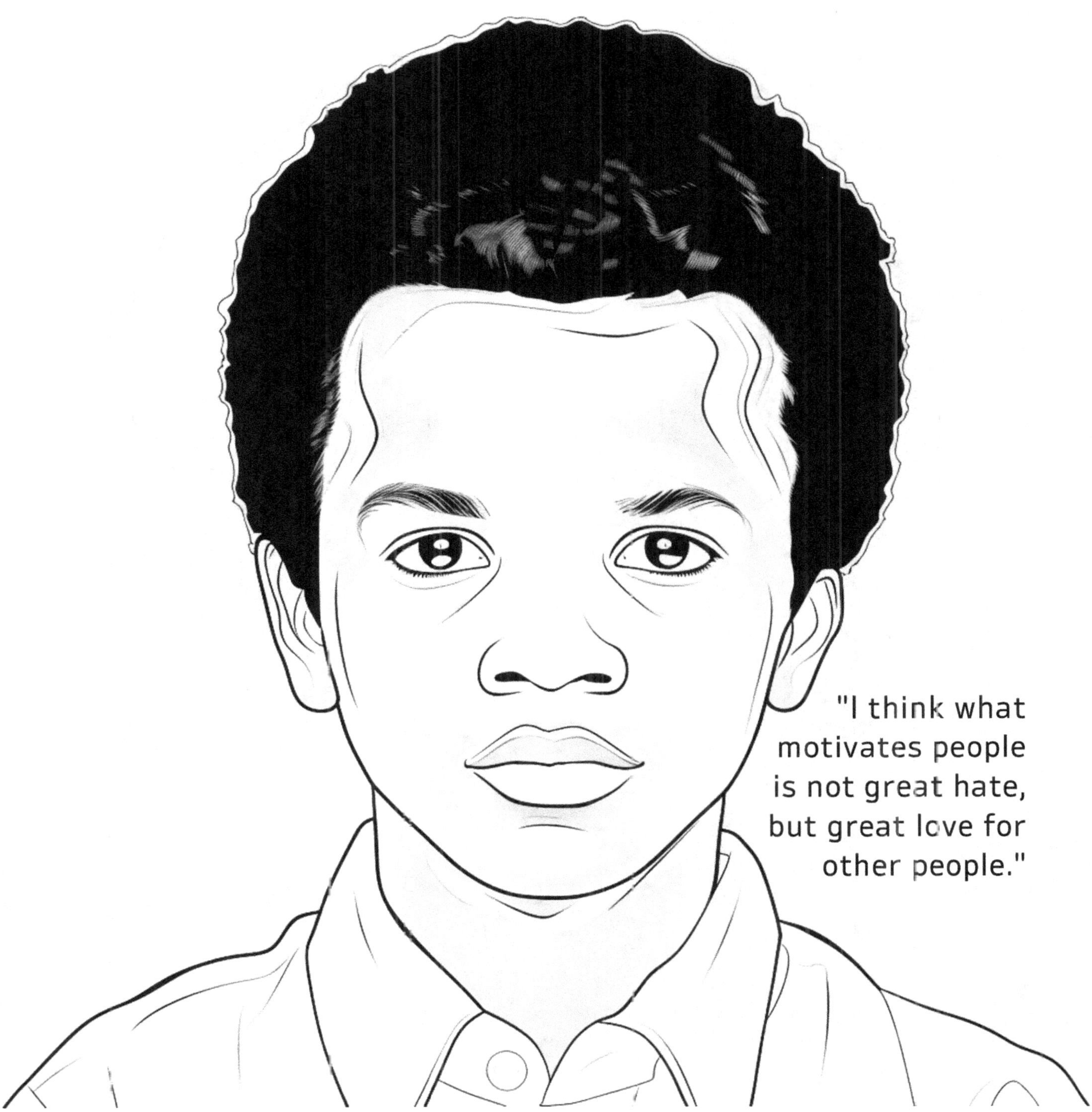

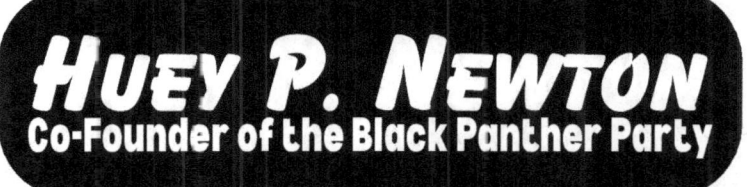

"I think what
motivates people
is not great hate,
but great love for
other people."

Huey P. Newton (February 17, 1942 – August 22, 1989) was a co-founder and leader of the Black Panther Party, a revolutionary socialist organization that fought for Black self-defense, community empowerment, and social justice. Newton's ideas and writings, particularly his book "Revolutionary Suicide" (1973), continue to influence discussions on race, activism, and revolution. He advocated for armed self-defense as a means to combat police brutality and systemic oppression. Newton's leadership and contributions to the civil rights movement left a lassting impact on the struggle for Black liberation.

HUEY P. NEWTON
Co-Founder of the Black Panther Party

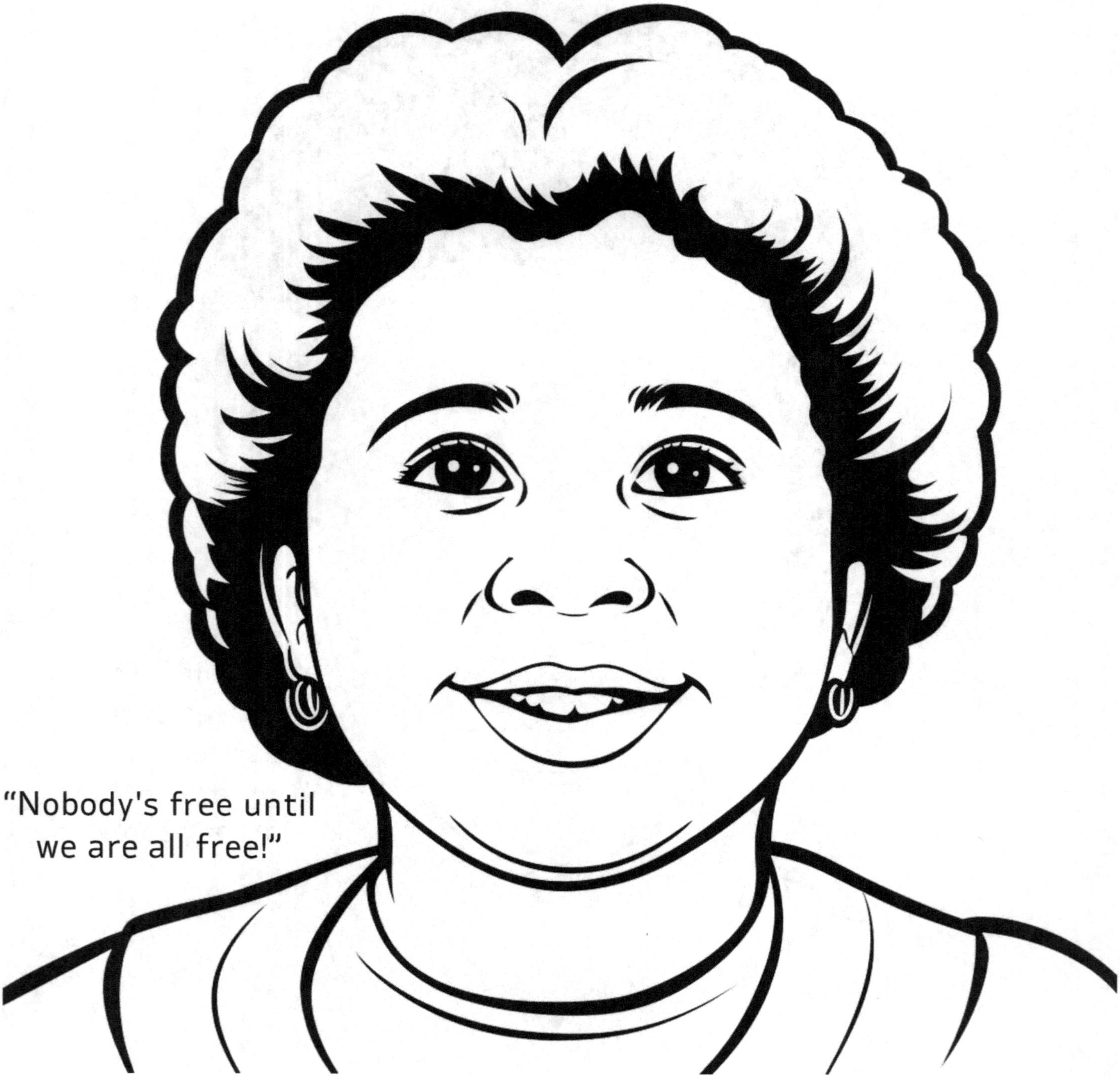

"Nobody's free until we are all free!"

Fannie Lou Hamer (October 6, 1917 – March 14, 1977) was a voting rights activist and a leader in the Civil Rights Movement. Hamer played a crucial role in organizing Mississippi's Freedom Summer and became known for her powerful speeches and testimonies about the challenges faced rby African Americans in the South. She co-founded the Mississippi Freedom Democratic Party, which challenged the all-white Democratic Party's exclusion of Black voters. Despite facing violent opposition and personal hardships, Hamer fought tirelessly for voting rights and racial justice.

2

FANNIE LOU HAMER
Voting Rights Activist, Civil Rights Leader

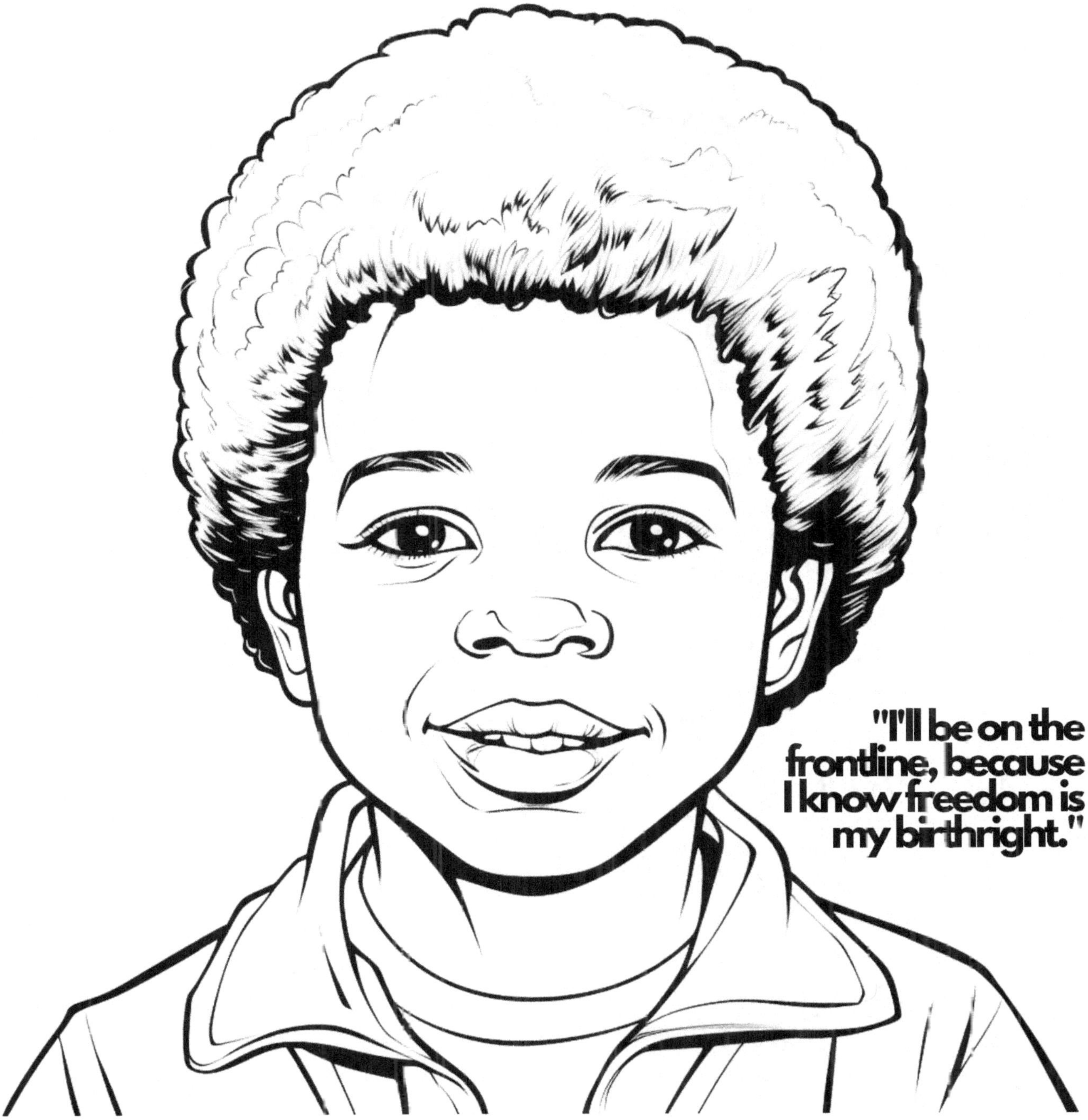

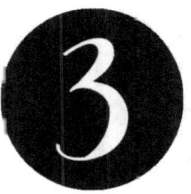

"I'll be on the frontline, because I know freedom is my birthright."

Bobby Hutton (April 21, 1950 – April 6, 1968) was a member of the Black Panther Party and one of its youngest recruits. He became a symbol of youthful resistance against racial injustice and police brutality. Hutton was involved in community service programs organized by the Black Panther Party and advocated for social change. Tragically, he was killed by law enforcement officers during a confrontation, further fueling the movement against systemic oppression and racism.

BOBBY HUTTON
Member of the Black Panther Party

3

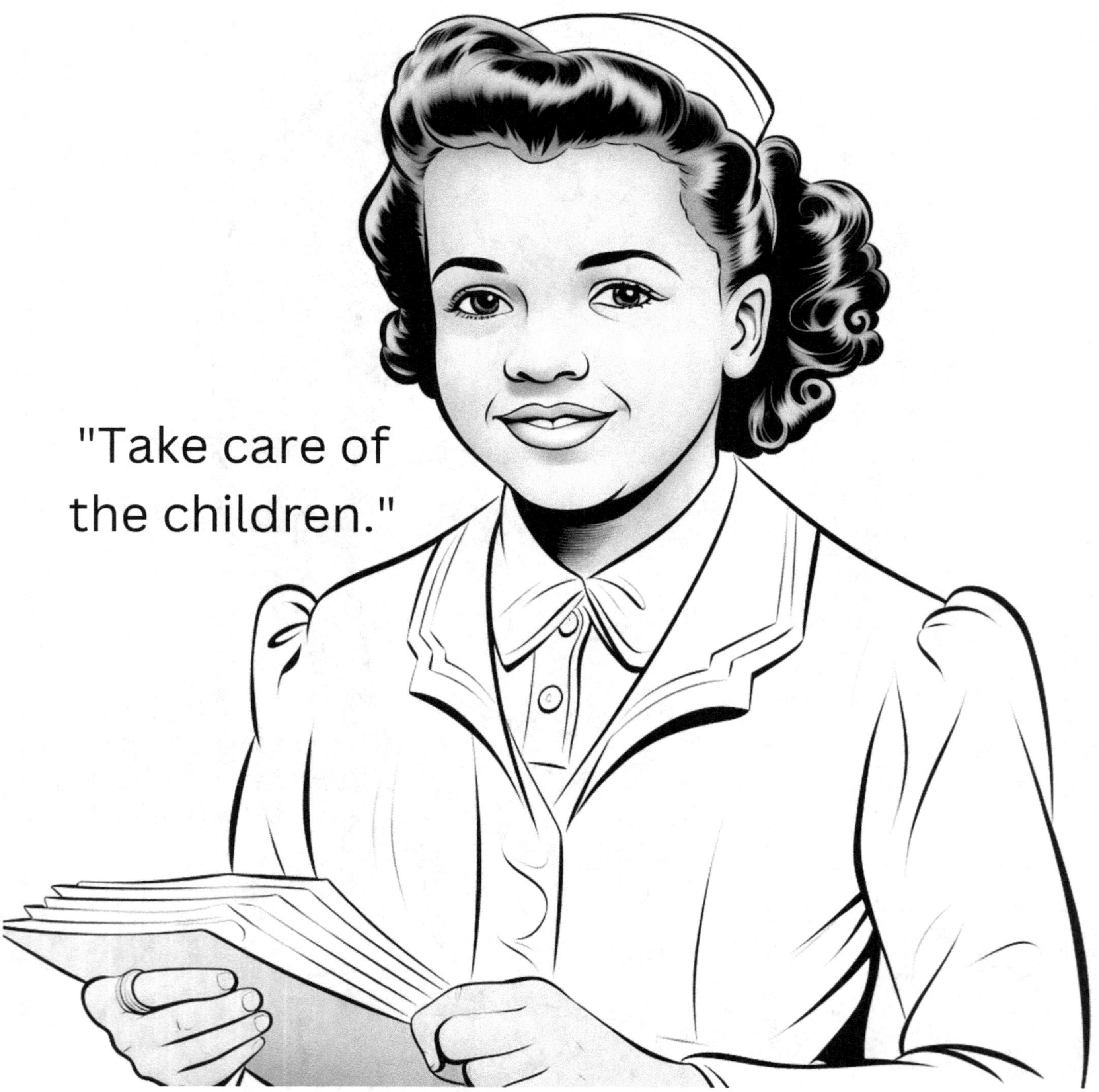

"Take care of
the children."

Henrietta Lacks (August 1, 1920 – October 4, 1951) was an African-American woman whose cells were taken without her knowledge or consent and became the source of the HeLa cell line, which has been instrumental in numerous medical advancements and research breakthroughs. Her cells, known for their remarkable ability to reproduce and survive, have been used in medical research, including the development of the polio vaccine and advancements in cancer treatments. Lacks' story raised important ethical questions regarding patient consent and the use of human tissues for scientific purposes.

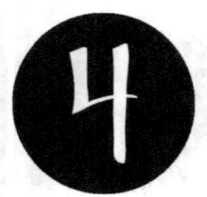

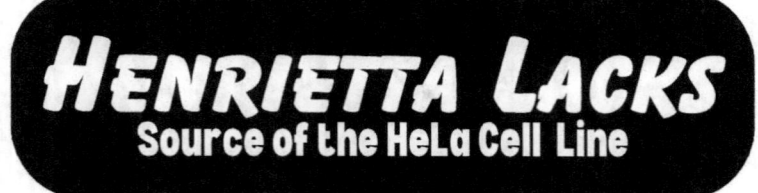

HENRIETTA LACKS
Source of the HeLa Cell Line

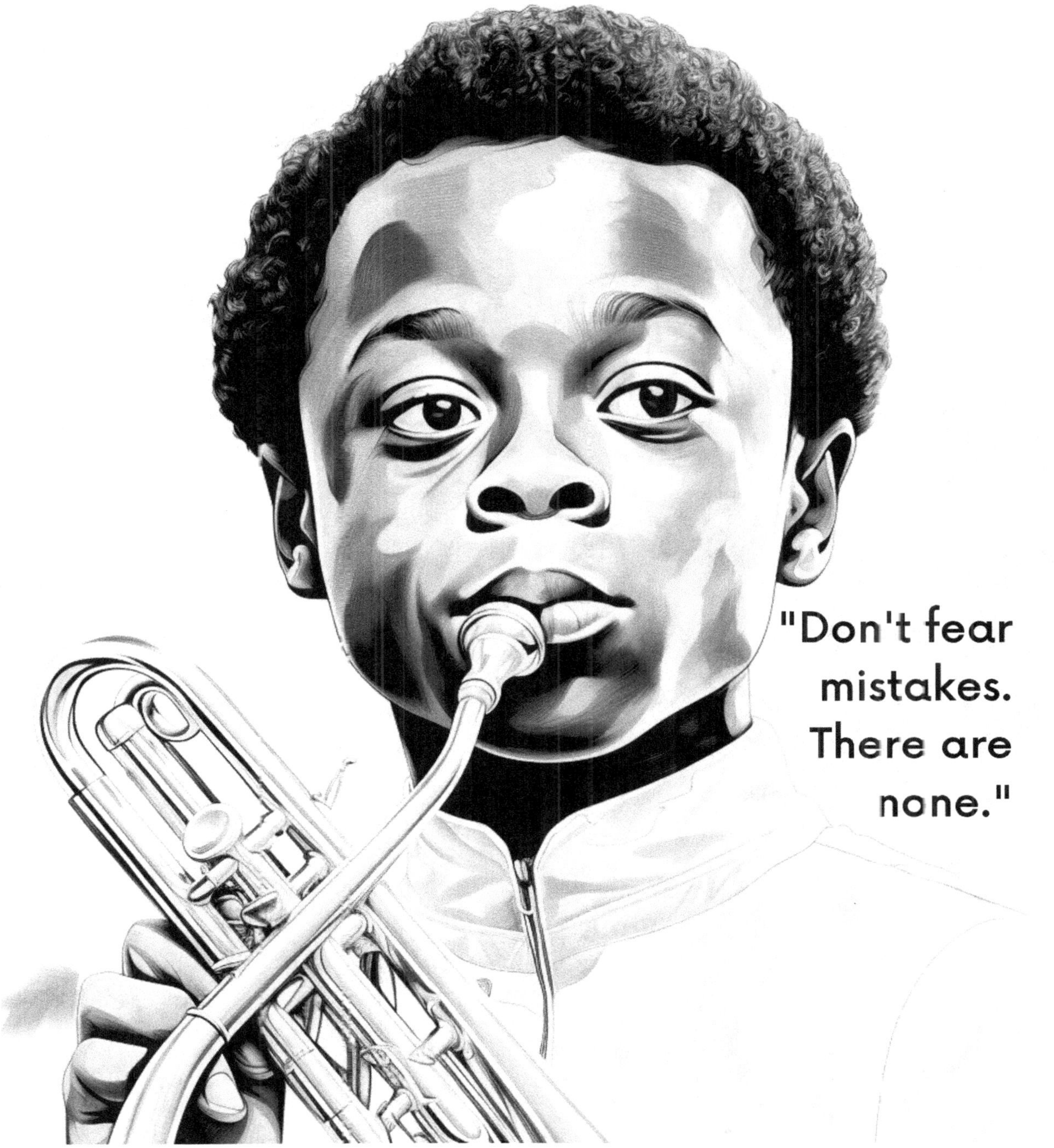

"Don't fear mistakes. There are none."

Miles Davis (Miles Dewey Davis III) (May 26, 1926 – September 28, 1991) was an American jazz trumpeter, bandleader, and composer. Born in Alton, Illinois, Davis began his musical journey at an early age, learning to play the trumpet by the age of 13. Davis was a trailblazing trumpeter who revolutionized jazz several times over during his career. Davis was an outspoken advocate for civil rights and played a significant role in breaking racial barriers in the jazz world. He refused to perform in venues that upheld segregation and used his influence to support fellow African American musicians.

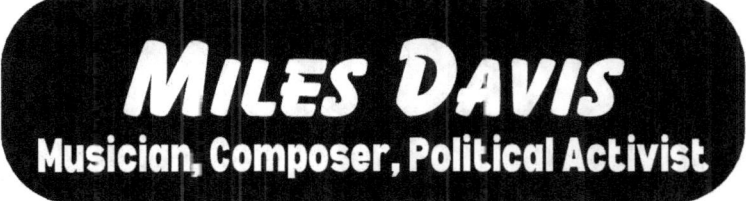

MILES DAVIS
Musician, Composer, Political Activist

"The only tired I was, was tired of giving in."

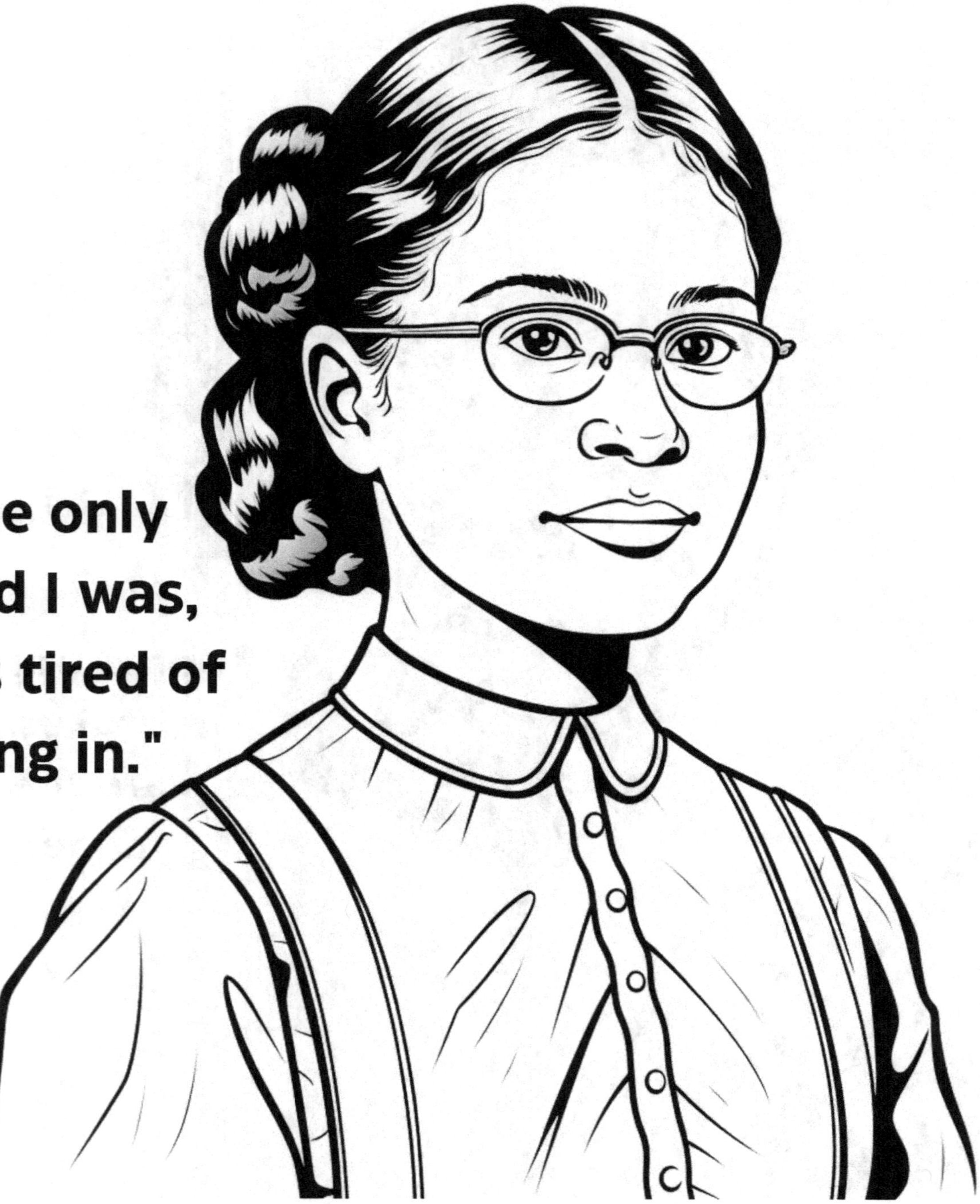

Rosa Parks (Rosa Louise McCauley Parks) (February 4, 1913 – October 24, 2005) was a prominent civil rights activist known for her pivotal role in the Montgomery Bus Boycott in 1955. By refusing to give up her seat to a white passenger on a Montgomery bus, Parks sparked a nonviolent protest that lasted over a year and ultimately led to the desegregation of public transportation in the city. Parks' act of resistance became a symbol of the civil rights movement and inspired countless others to join the struggle against racial segregation and discrimination.

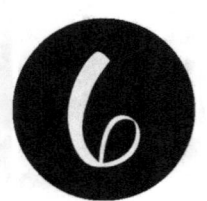

6

ROSA PARKS
Civil Rights Activist

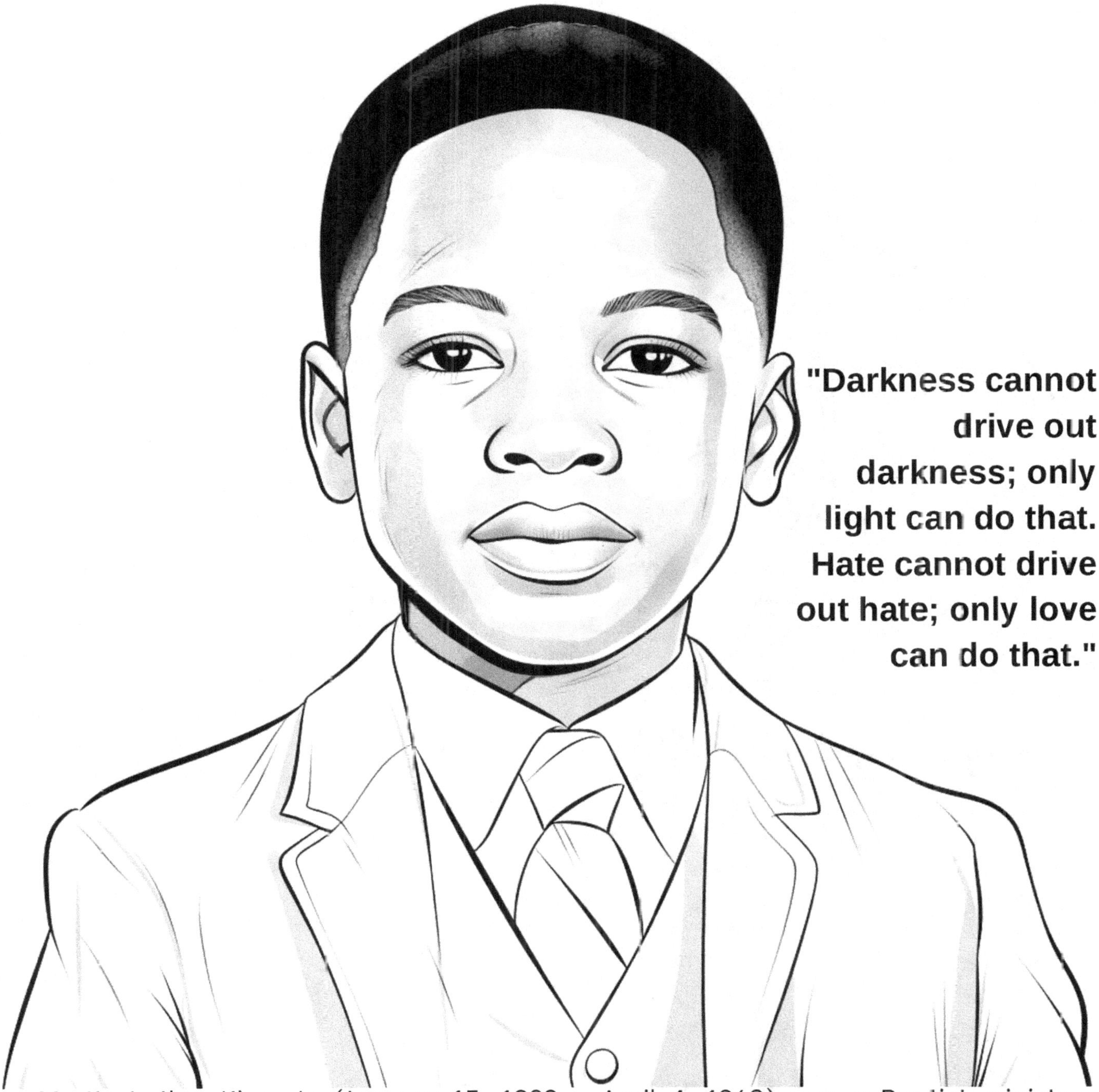

"Darkness cannot drive out darkness; only light can do that. Hate cannot drive out hate; only love can do that."

Martin Luther King, Jr. (January 15, 1929 – April 4, 1968) was a Baptist minister, activist, and the most prominent leader of the civil rights movement in the United States. Known for his advocacy of nonviolent protest, King played a key role in organizing and leading civil rights campaigns, including the Montgomery Bus Boycott and the March on Washington where he delivered his iconic "I Have a Dream" speech, calling for an end to racism and equality for all. King's tireless efforts and powerful speeches contributed to the passage of key legislation, including the Civil Rights Act of 1964 and the Voting Rights Act of 1965.

MARTIN LUTHER KING, JR. 7
Minister, Civil Rights Leader

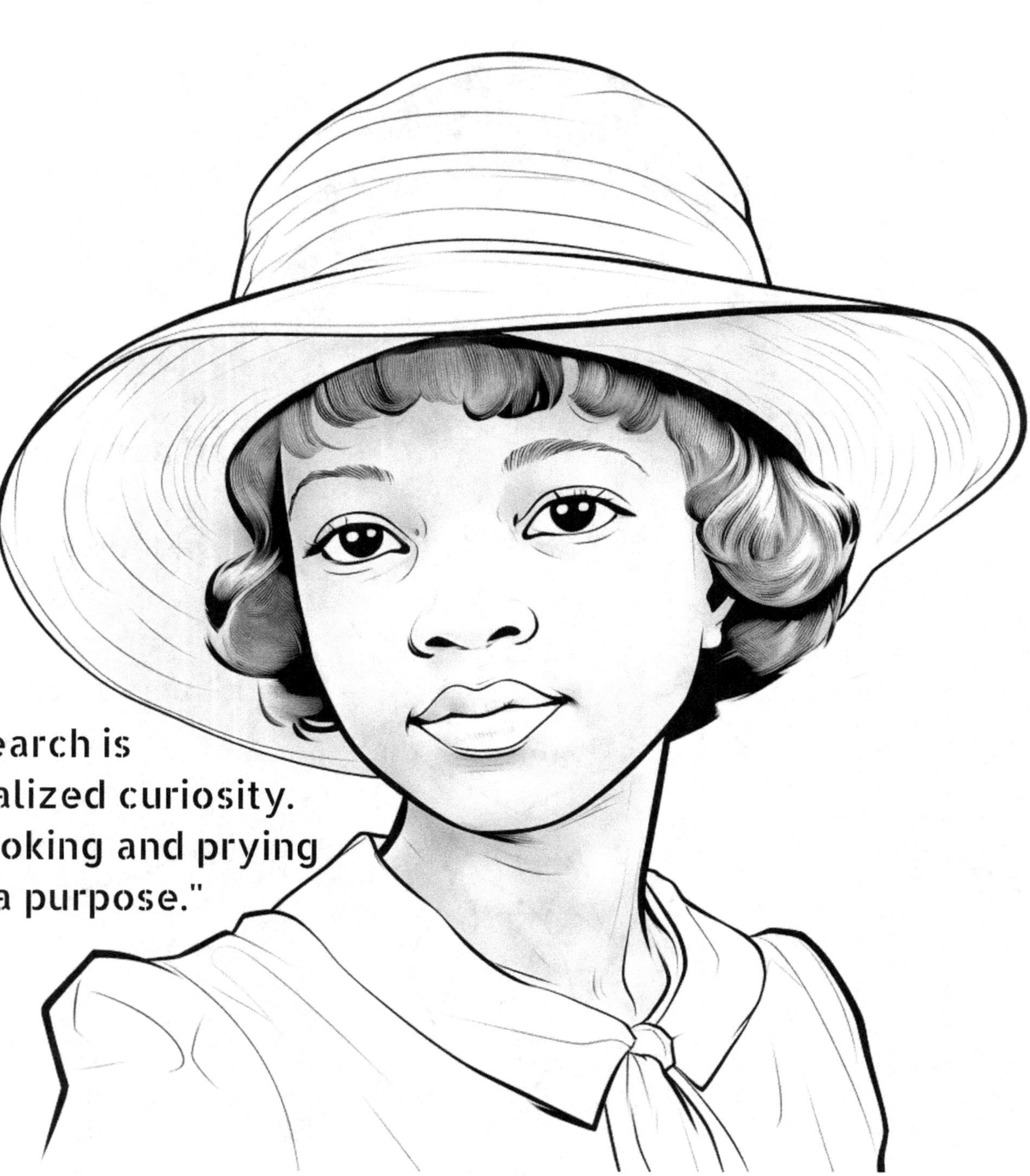

"Research is
formalized curiosity.
It is poking and prying
with a purpose."

Zora Neale Hurston (January 7, 1891 – January 28, 1960) was an influential writer and anthropologist associated with the Harlem Renaissance. Her writings, such as the novel "Their Eyes Were Watching God" (1937), explored the experiences of African Americans, particularly women, in the early 20th century. Hurston's works celebrated the richness of Black culture and folklore, challenging prevailing stereotypes. As an anthropologist, she conducted groundbreaking research on African-American folk traditions in the United States and the Caribbean, documenting the cultural heritage of Black communities.

8 ZORA NEALE HURSTON
Writer, Author, Anthropologist

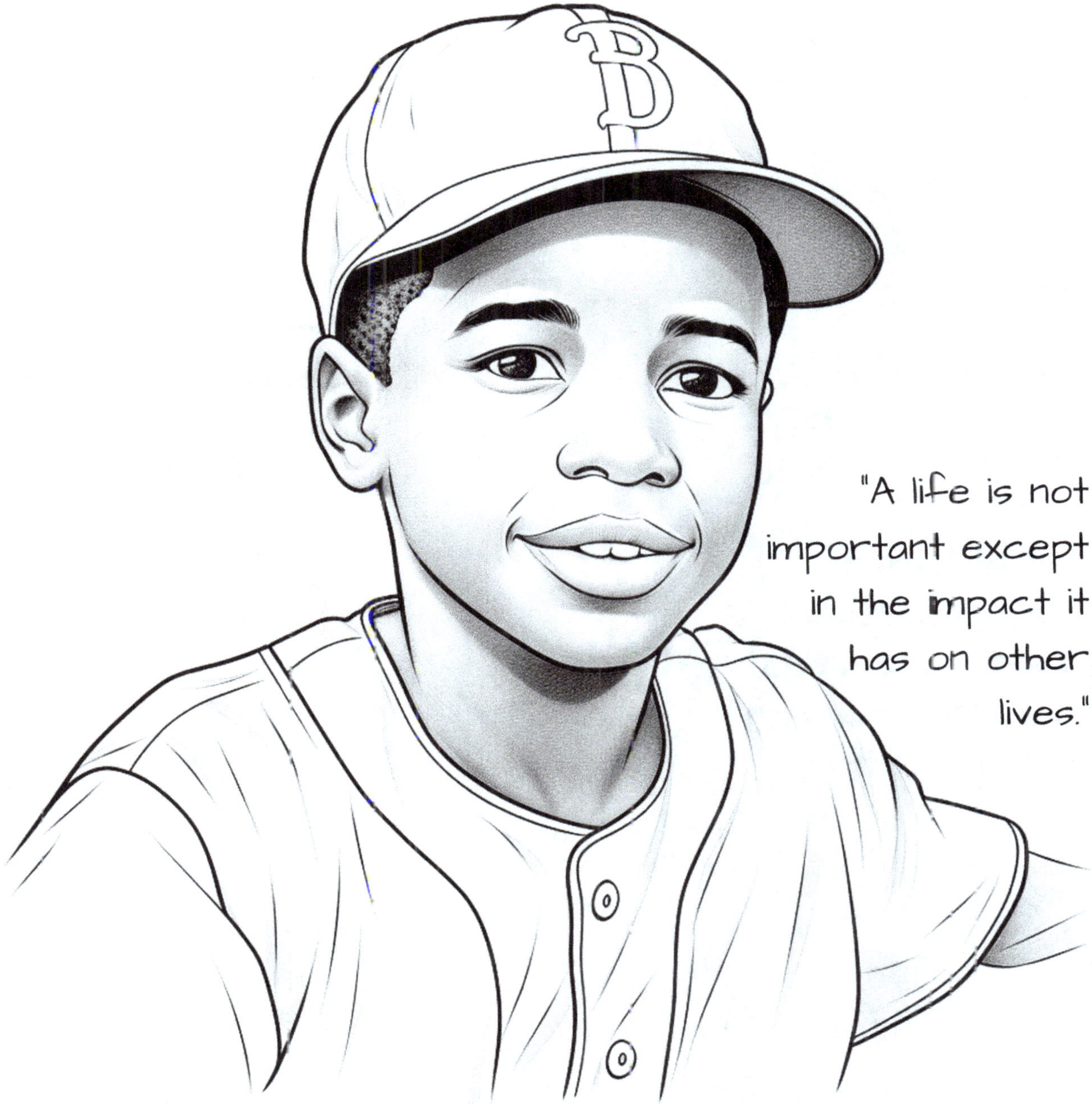

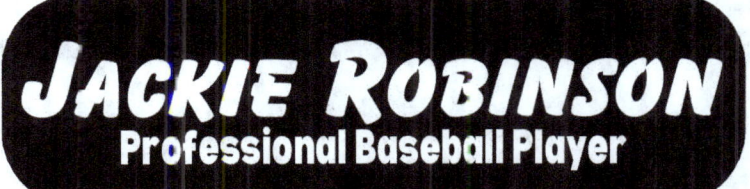

"A life is not important except in the impact it has on other lives."

Jackie Robinson (Jack Roosevelt Robinson) (January 31, 1919 – October 24, 1972) was a professional baseball player who became the first African-American to play in Major League Baseball (MLB) in the modern era. Breaking the color barrier in 1947, Robinson faced racial discrimination and hostility but displayed remarkable talent and resilience on the field. His achievements as a player and his courage in the face of adversity paved the way for the desegregation of professional sports and became an inspiration for the civil rights movement. Robinson's legacy extends far beyond baseball, symbolizing the fight for racial equality and social progress.

JACKIE ROBINSON
Professional Baseball Player

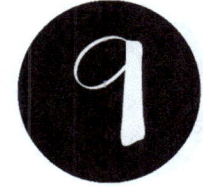

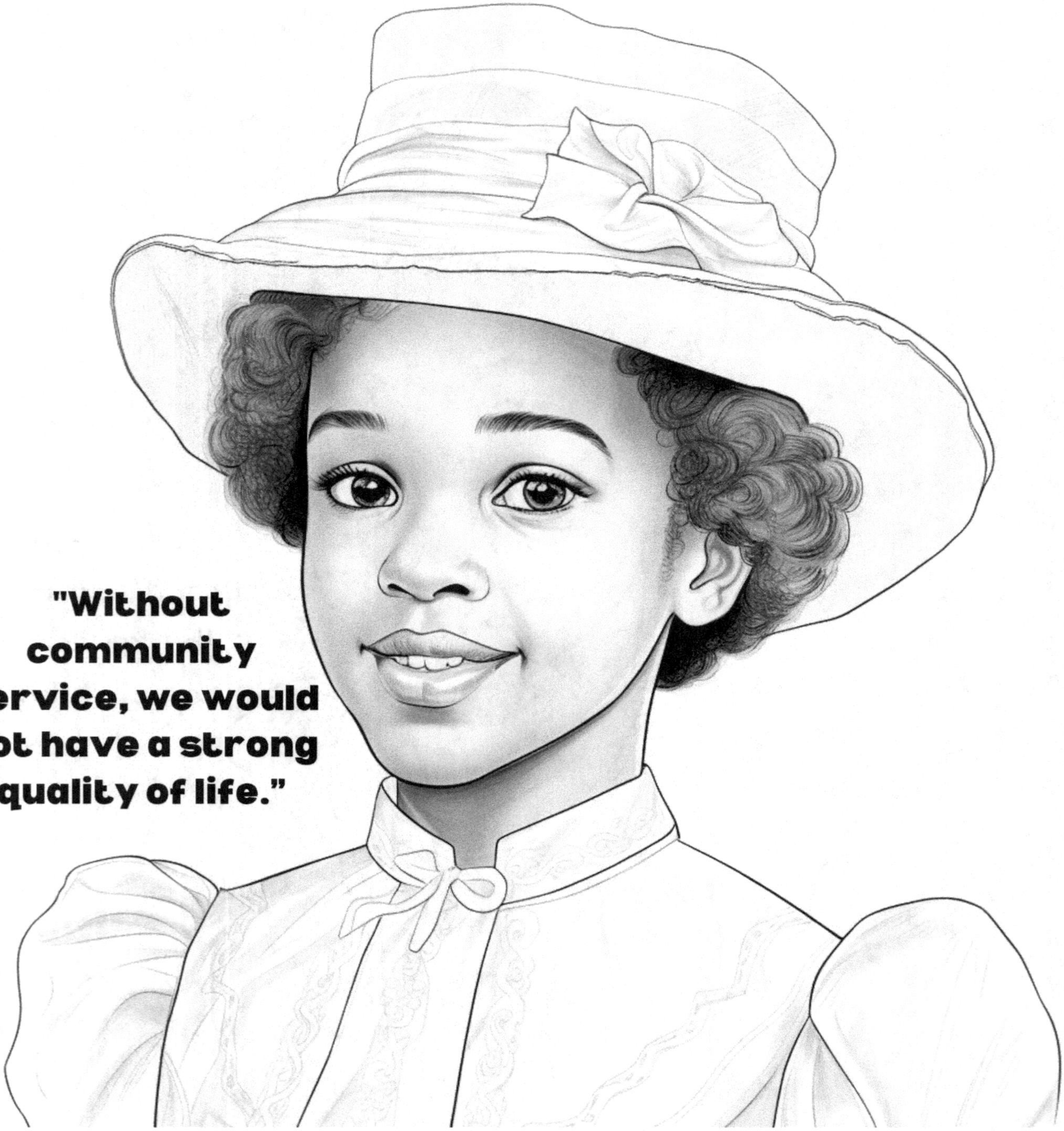

"Without community service, we would not have a strong quality of life."

Dorothy Height (March 24, 1912 – April 20, 2010) was a women's rights and civil rights activist who dedicated her life to fighting for gender and racial equality. Height served as the president of the National Council of Negro Women for over 40 years, advocating for issues such as education, employment, and reproductive rights. She worked alongside prominent civil rights leaders and was instrumental in organizing the 1963 March on Washington. Height's tireless efforts and leadership helped advance the rights of African-American women and shaped the progress of the civil rights movement.

10

DOROTHY HEIGHT
Women's Rights and Civil Rights Activist

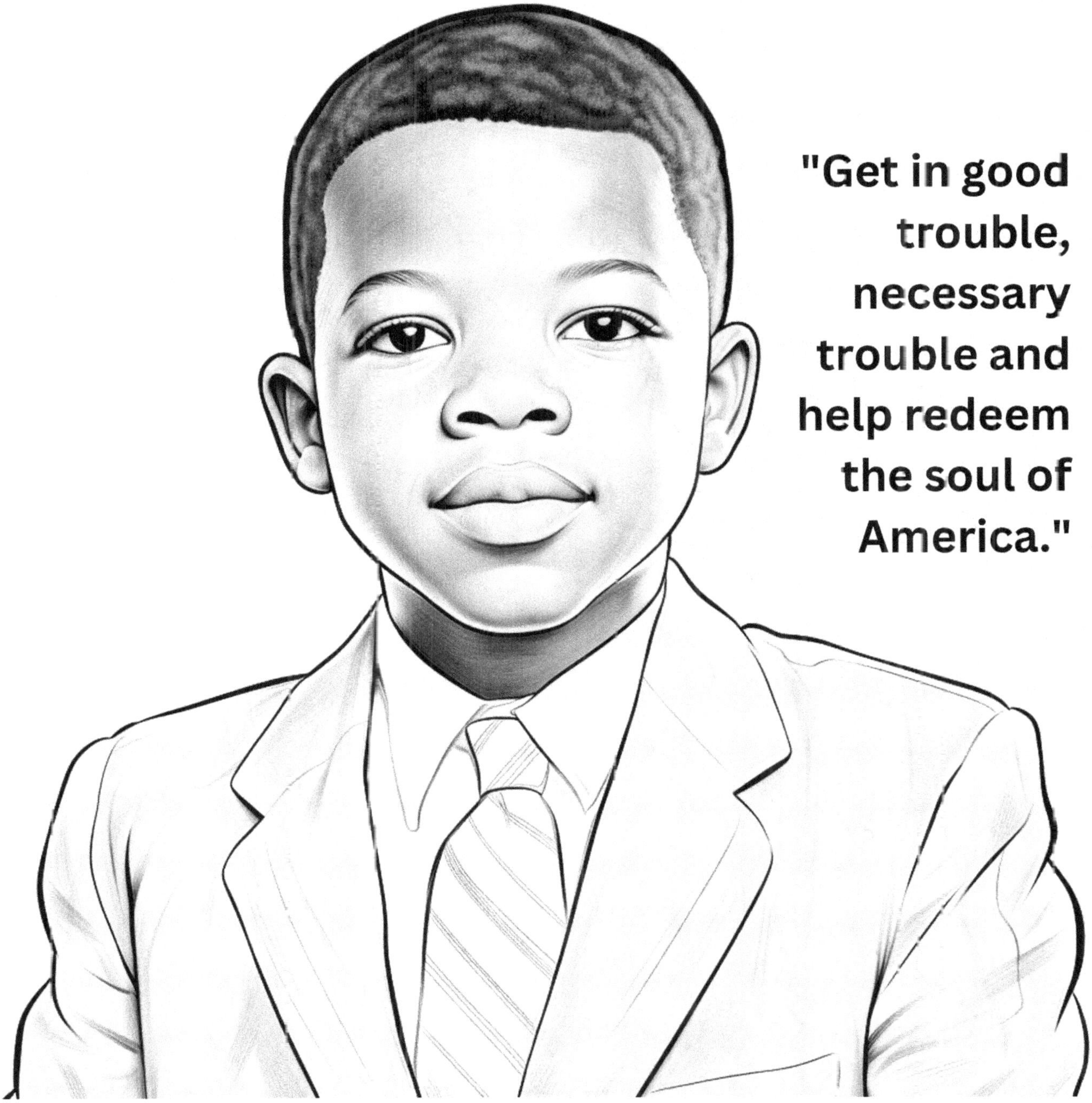

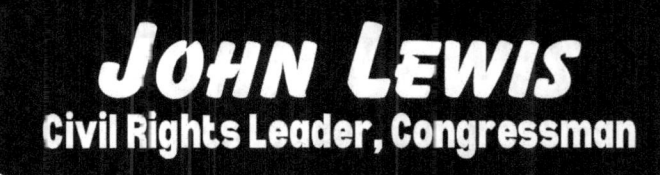

"Get in good trouble, necessary trouble and help redeem the soul of America."

John Lewis (February 21, 1940 – July 17, 2020) was a civil rights leader, congressman, and advocate for social justice. As one of the "Big Six" leaders of the civil rights movement, Lewis played a pivotal role in organizing and participating in various protests and marches, including the historic March on Washington in 1963. He endured violent attacks and arrests while advocating for voting rights and equality. Lewis later served in the United States House of Representatives for Georgia's 5th congressional district for over three decades, continuing his work to advance civil rights and social change.

JOHN LEWIS
Civil Rights Leader, Congressman

"Ain't I a Woman?"

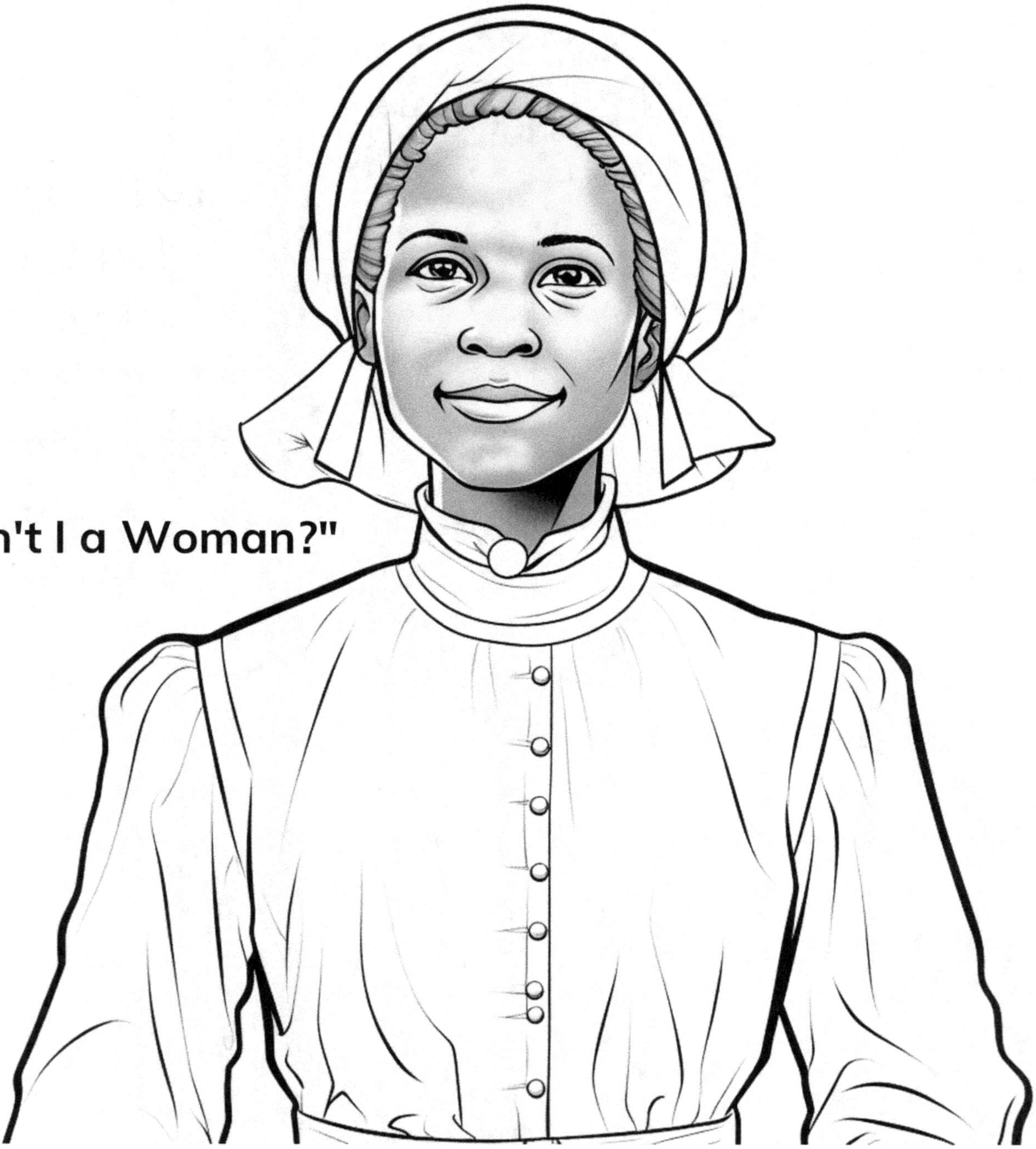

Sojourner Truth (Isabella Baumfree) (c. 1797 – November 26, 1883) was an abolitionist and women's rights advocate. Born into slavery, she escaped to freedom and became one of the most prominent voices for both the abolition of slavery and women's rights. Truth delivered her famous speech, "Ain't I a Woman?" in 1851 at the Women's Convention in Ohio, challenging the prevailing stereotypes and advocating for the equal rights of Black women. Her courageous activism and powerful oratory skills made her a respected figure in the fight for justice and equality.

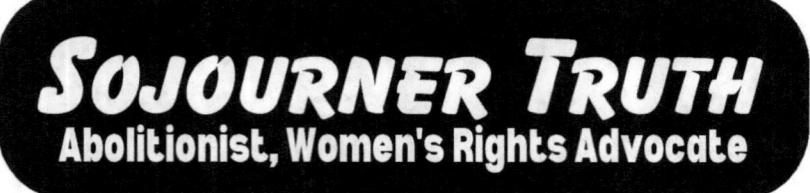

SOJOURNER TRUTH
Abolitionist, Women's Rights Advocate

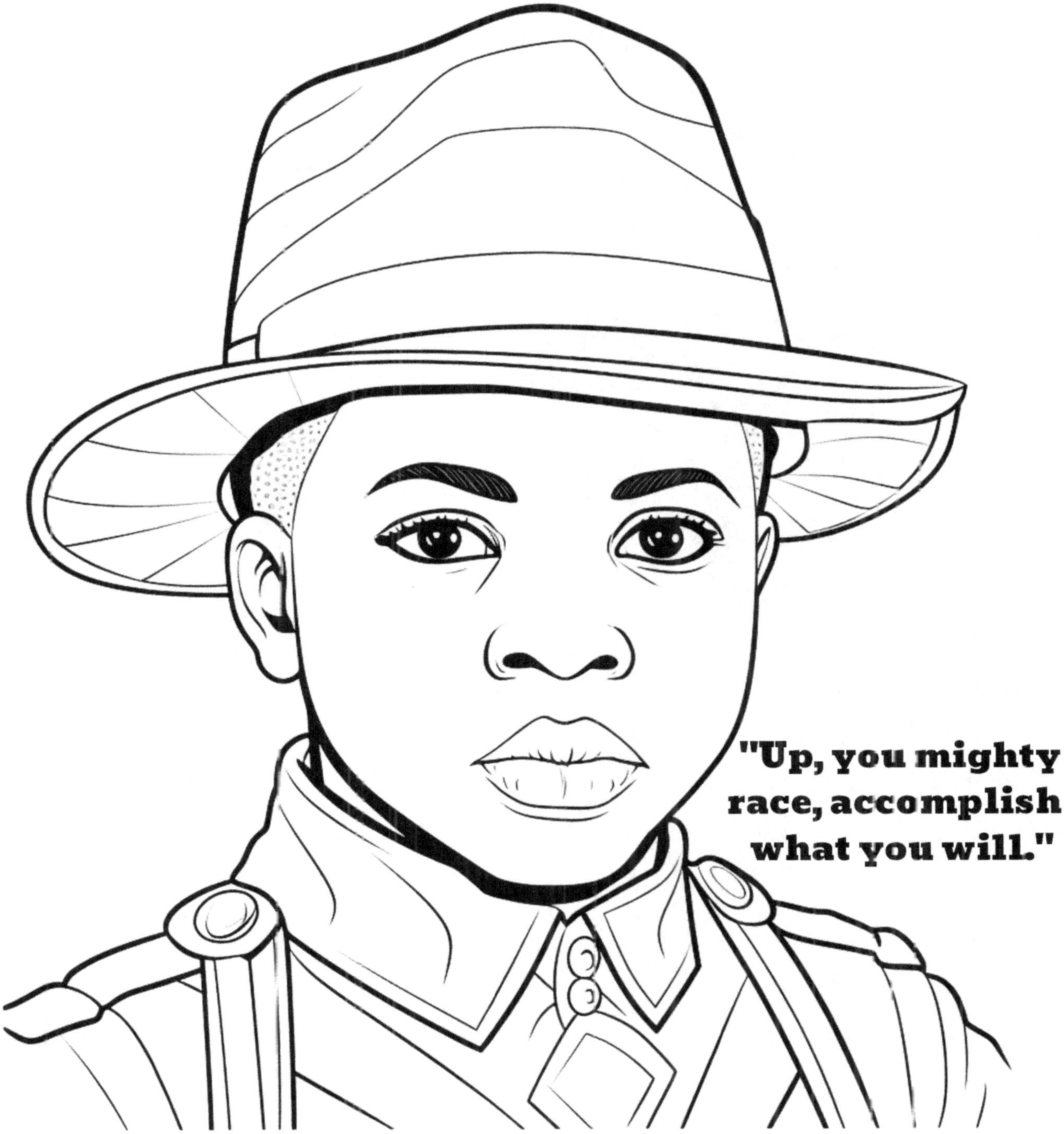

"Up, you mighty race, accomplish what you will."

Marcus Garvey (August 17, 1887 – June 10, 1940) was a Jamaican-born political leader and activist who founded the Universal Negro Improvement Association (UNIA) and the African Communities League. Garvey promoted Black nationalism, economic self-sufficiency, and a strong sense of racial pride. He advocated for the repatriation of African descendants to Africa and called for the establishment of an independent Black nation. Garvey's ideas and teachings continue to resonate with various Black nationalist movements and the Pan-African movement.

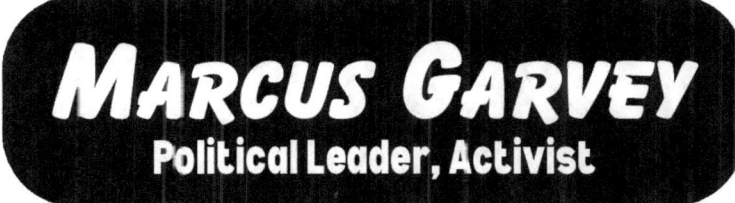

MARCUS GARVEY
Political Leader, Activist

13

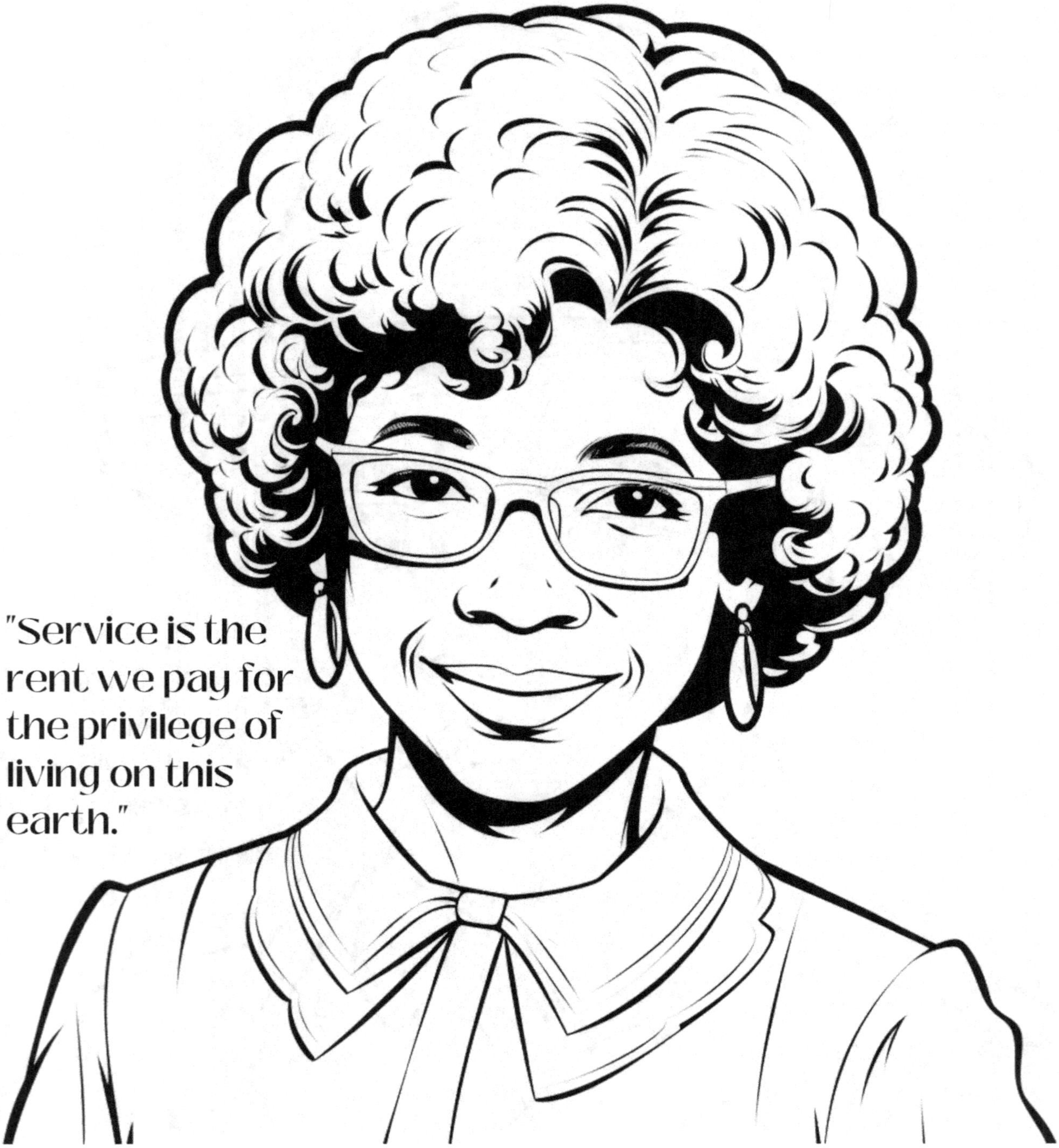

"Service is the rent we pay for the privilege of living on this earth."

Shirley Chisholm (November 30, 1924 – January 1, 2005) was a trailblazing politician and activist who became the first African-American woman elected to the United States Congress. She served in the House of Representatives from 1969 to 1983. Chisholm was a fierce advocate for the rights of marginalized communities, including African Americans, women, and the poor. She sought to bring attention to issues such as racial and gender inequality, education, and social welfare. Chisholm also made history when she ran for the Democratic Party's presidential nomination in 1972, becoming the first Black woman to do so.

14

SHIRLEY CHISHOLM
Politician, Activist

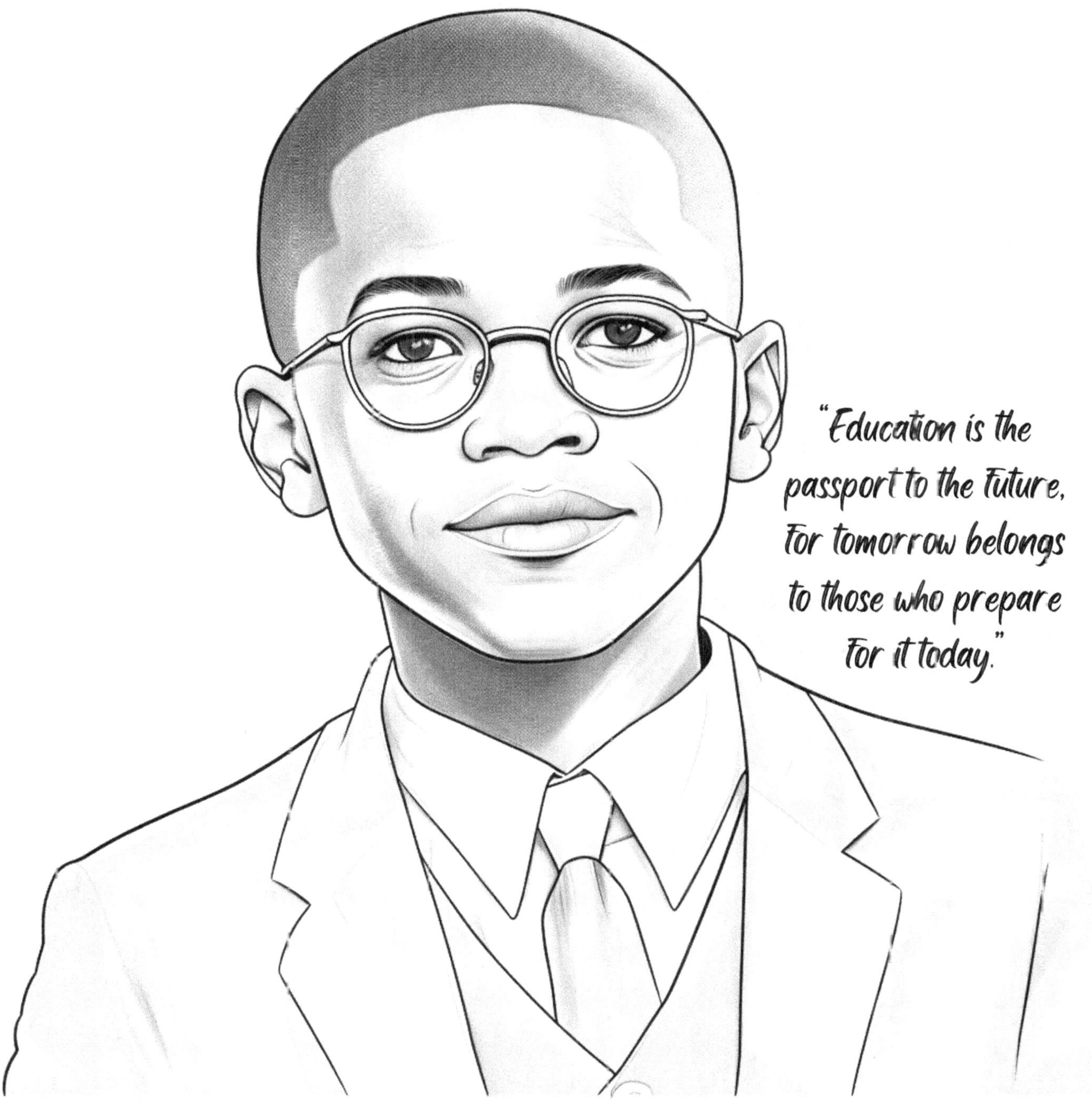

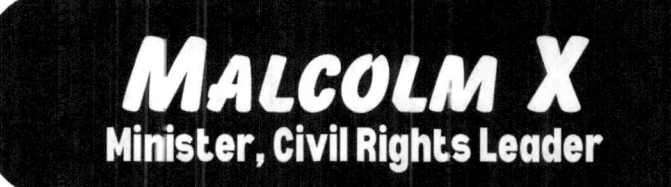

"Education is the passport to the future, for tomorrow belongs to those who prepare for it today."

Malcolm X (Malcolm Little, also known as El-Hajj Malik El-Shabazz) (May 19, 1925 – February 21, 1965) was a prominent civil rights leader, minister, and advocate for Black empowerment. He initially gained attention as a spokesperson for the Nation of Islam, advocating for racial separation and self-defense. After leaving the Nation of Islam, Malcolm X embraced a more inclusive vision of civil rights and racial equality. He became a powerful voice for Black liberation, challenging systemic racism and oppression. Malcolm X's speeches and writings, including his autobiography, continue to inspire and provoke discussions on race and identity.

MALCOLM X
Minister, Civil Rights Leader

15

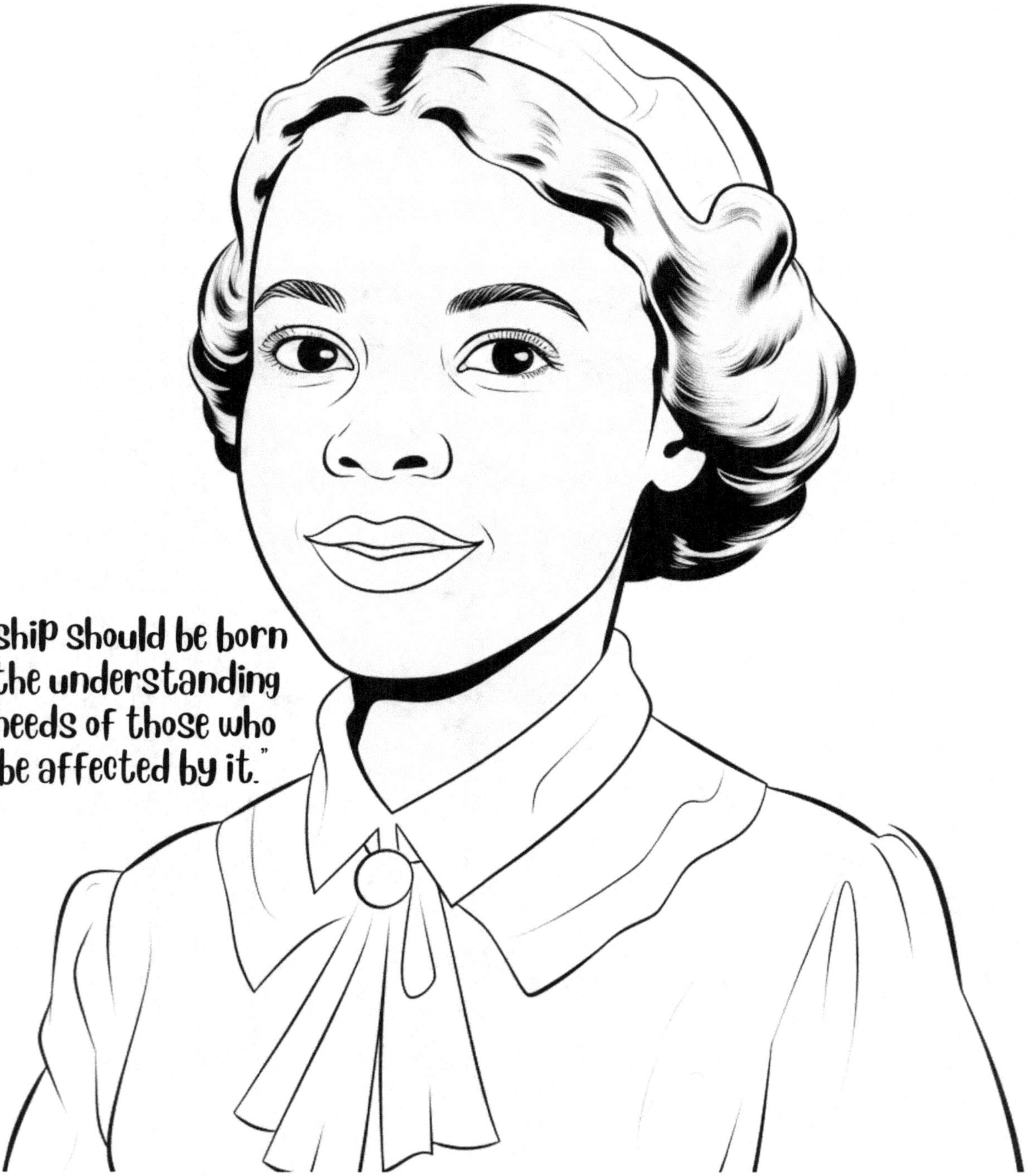

"Leadership should be born out of the understanding of the needs of those who would be affected by it."

Marian Anderson (February 27, 1897 – April 8, 1993) was a contralto singer who achieved international acclaim for her powerful voice and performances. Anderson's talent transcended racial barriers, and she became the first African-American to perform at the Metropolitan Opera in 1955. Her iconic performance on the steps of the Lincoln Memorial in 1939, after being denied the opportunity to perform at Constitution Hall due to racial segregation, drew attention to the struggle for civil rights. Anderson used her voice to inspire and advocate for equality throughout her career.

MARIAN ANDERSON
Contralto Singer

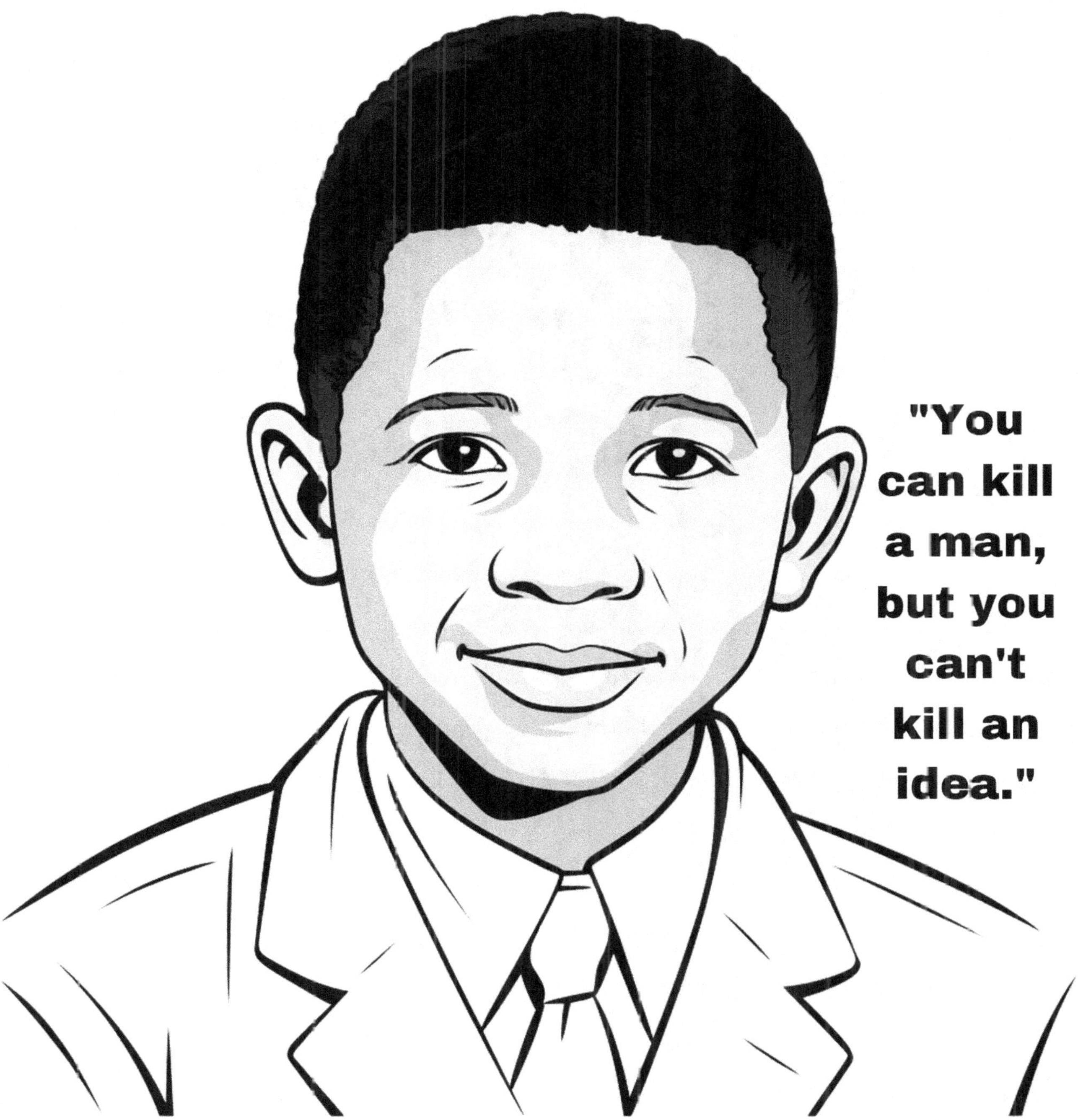

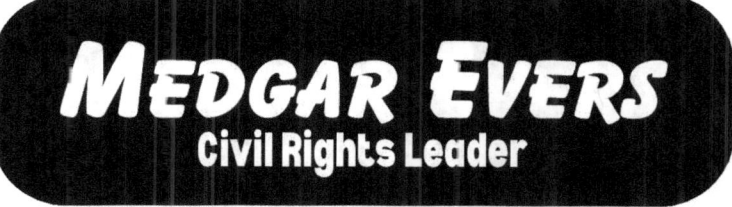

"You
can kill
a man,
but you
can't
kill an
idea."

Medgar Evers (July 2, 1925 – June 12, 1963) was an African-American civil rights activist and leader of the NAACP in Mississippi. Evers dedicated his life to fighting for racial equality and voting rights. He organized protests and voter registration drives and worked to investigate and bring attention to cases of racial violence and discrimination. Tragically, Evers was assassinated outside his home in 1963, becoming a martyr for the civil rights movement. His death and the subsequent trial of his killer brought national attention to the struggle for equal rights and contributed to the passage of the Civil Rights Act of 1964.

MEDGAR EVERS
Civil Rights Leader

17

"Just don't give up trying to do what you really want to do. Where there is love and inspiration, I don't think you can go wrong."

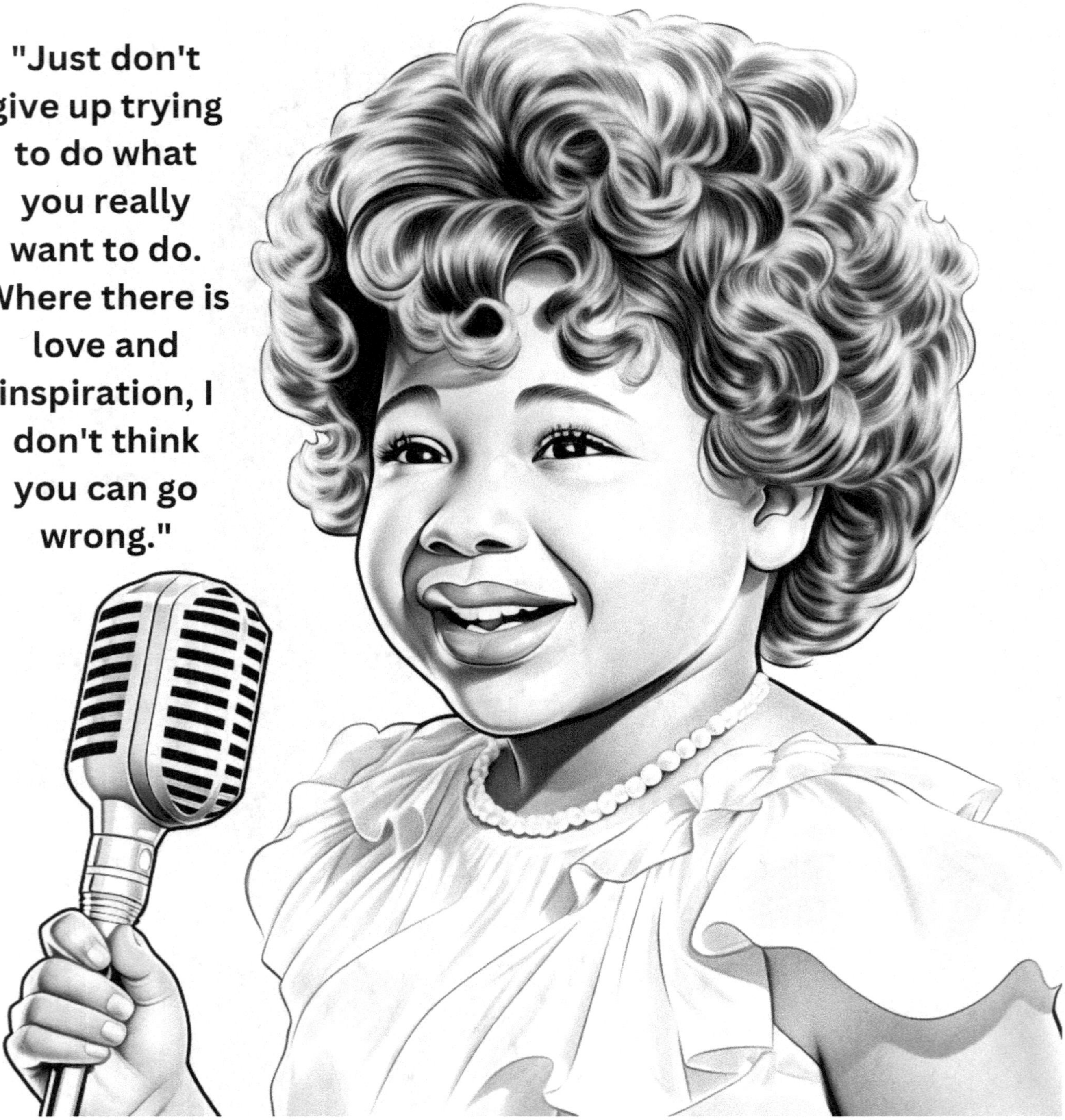

Ella Fitzgerald (April 25, 1917 – June 15, 1996) was a jazz singer often referred to as the "First Lady of Song." Her exceptional vocal talent, range, and improvisational skills made her one of the most influential jazz vocalists of all time. Fitzgerald's career spanned six decades, during which she recorded numerous hit songs and collaborated with jazz legends. Despite facing racial discrimination, she broke down barriers and became a beloved figure in the music industry. Fitzgerald's contributions to jazz and her timeless recordings continue to inspire generations of musicians.

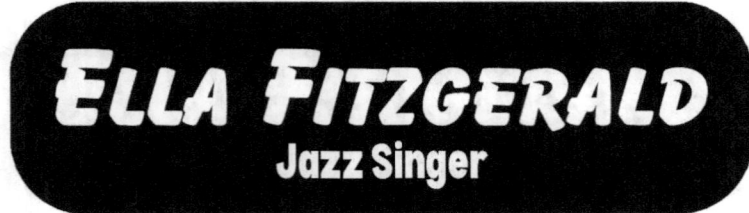

ELLA FITZGERALD
Jazz Singer

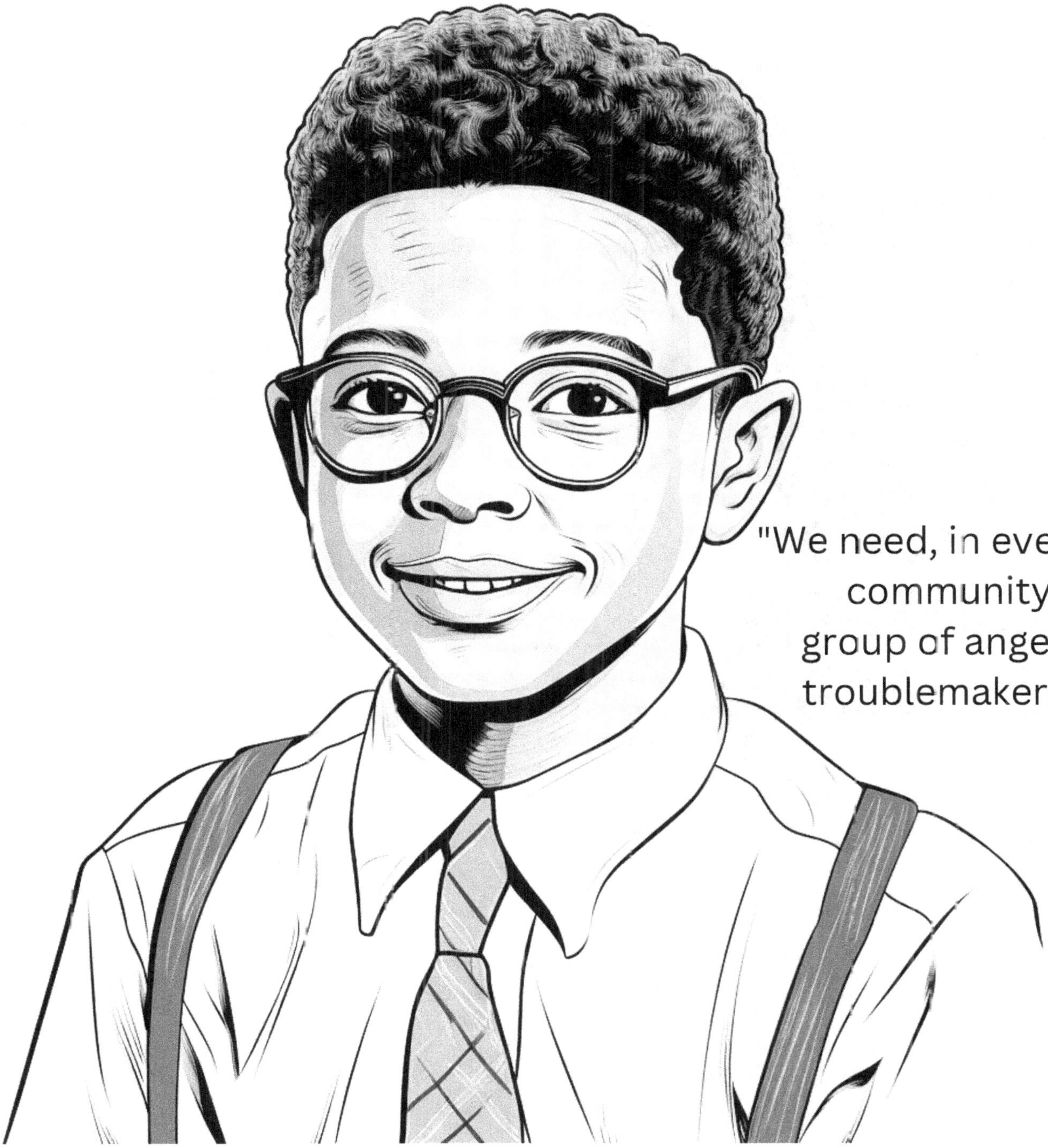

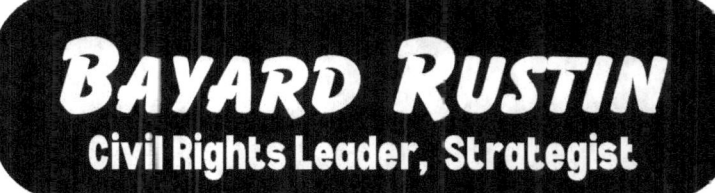

"We need, in every community, a group of angelic troublemakers."

Bayard Rustin (March 17, 1912 – August 24, 1987) was a civil rights leader and strategist who played a significant role in the American civil rights movement. He was a close advisor to Martin Luther King Jr. and a key organizer of the historic March on Washington in 1963. Rustin's commitment to nonviolent protest and his tireless efforts to promote equality and justice made him a central figure in the fight for civil rights. Despite facing discrimination as an openly gay man, Rustin continued his advocacy for social and economic justice throughout his life.

BAYARD RUSTIN
Civil Rights Leader, Strategist

"I believe that unarmed truth and unconditional love will have the final word in reality."

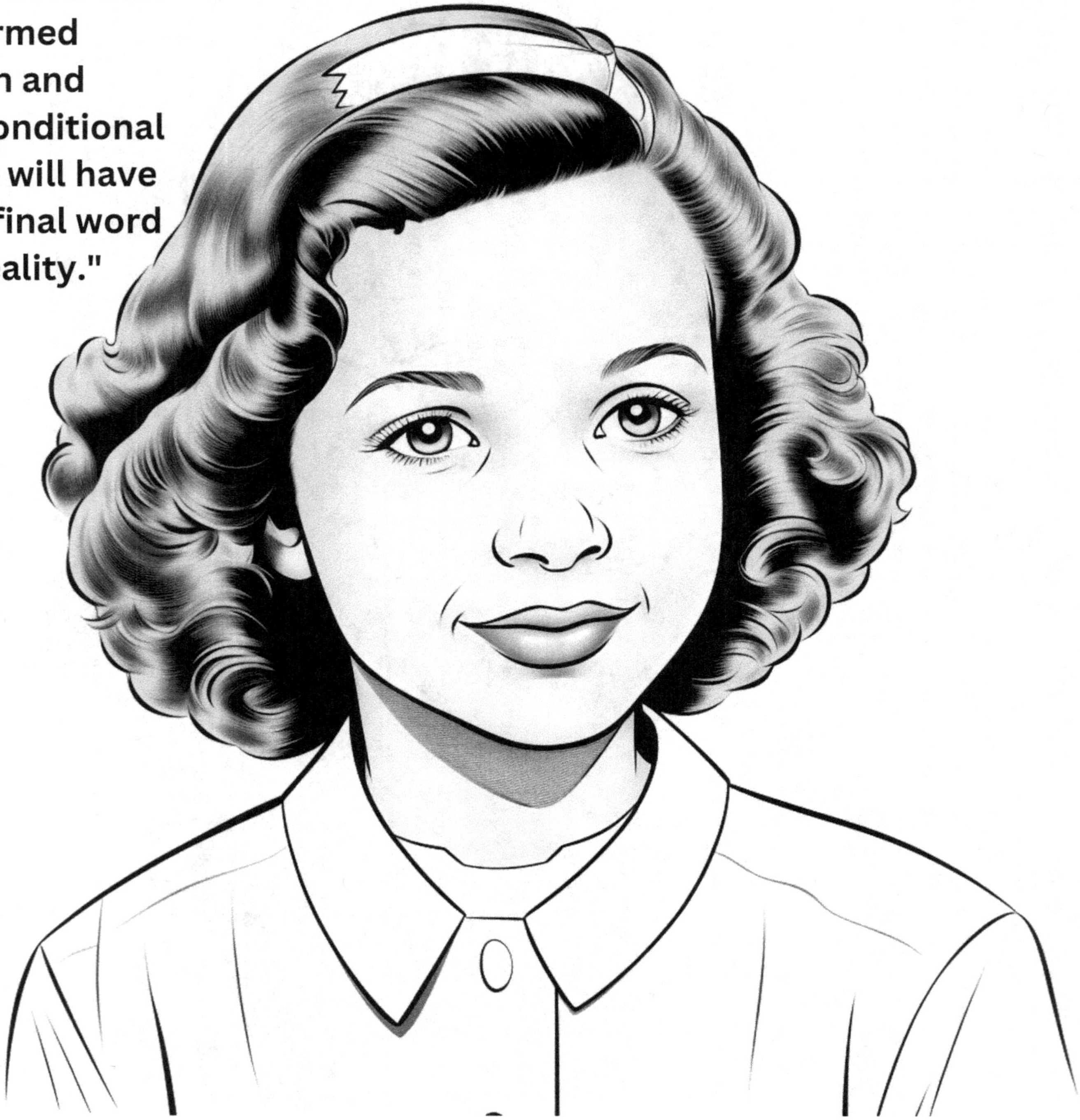

Diane Nash (born May 15, 1938) is a civil rights activist known for her work as a leader of the Nashville Student Movement and the Student Nonviolent Coordinating Committee (SNCC). Nash played a critical role in organizing the Freedom Rides, a series of integrated bus trips through the segregated South in 1961. She was a key strategist and advocate for nonviolent direct action, and her courage and commitment to justice helped bring attention to the injustices of segregation. Nash continues to be active in promoting equality and social justice.

20

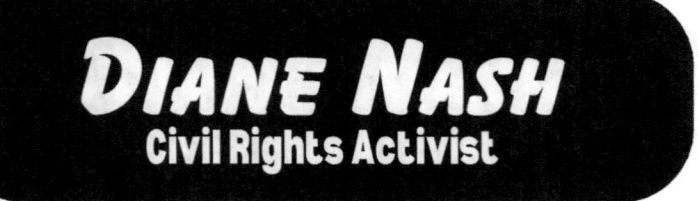
DIANE NASH
Civil Rights Activist

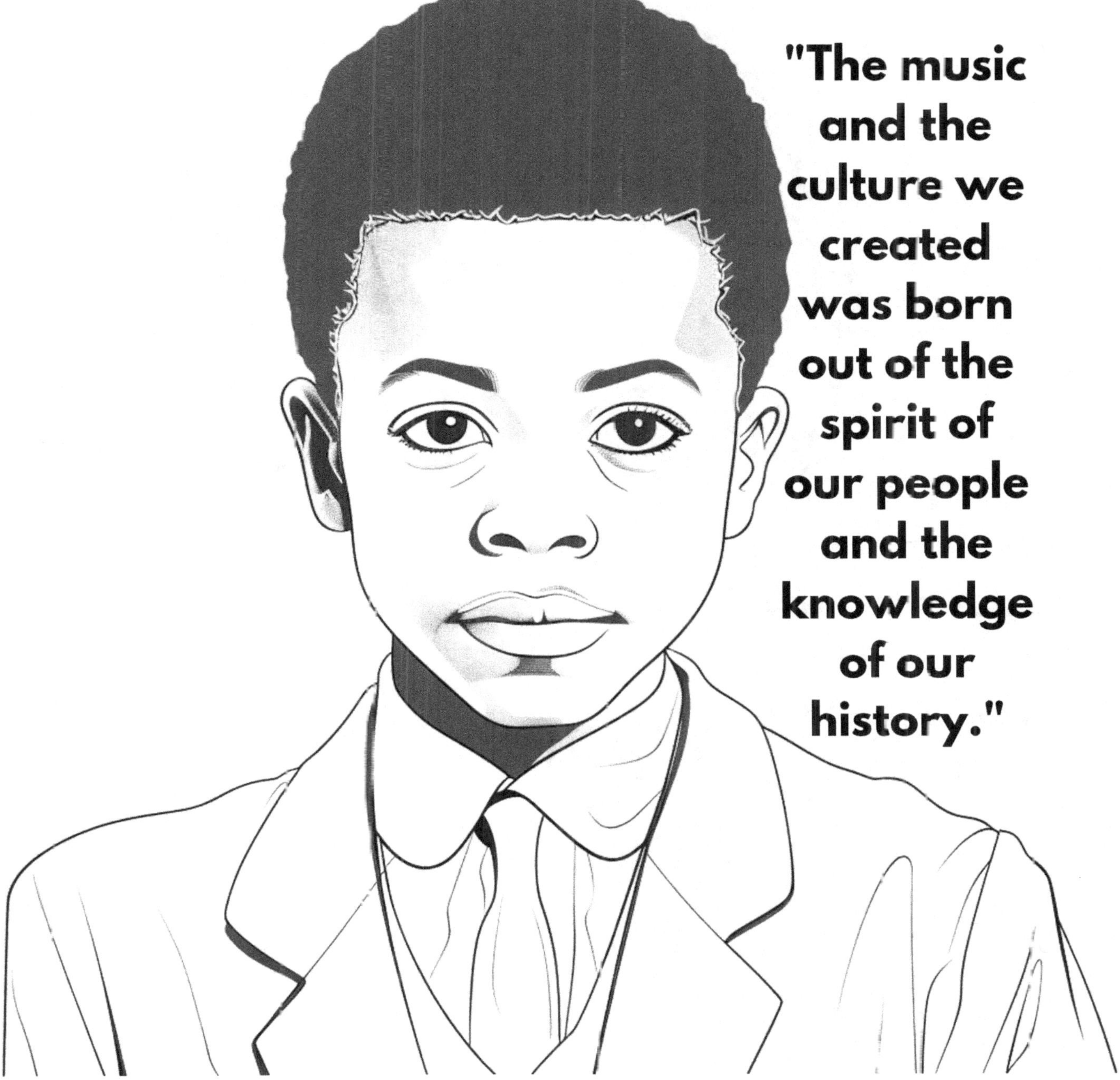

> "The music and the culture we created was born out of the spirit of our people and the knowledge of our history."

Amiri Baraka (LeRoi Jones) (October 7, 1934 – January 9, 2014), formerly known as LeRoi Jones, was an influential writer, poet, and playwright. His works, such as the play "Dutchman" (1964) and the poetry collection "Black Art" (1966), confronted issues of racism, cultural identity, and political radicalism. Baraka was associated with the Black Arts Movement, a cultural and artistic movement that sought to connect art with political activism. Throughout his career, Baraka used his writings to challenge societal norms and inspire social change.

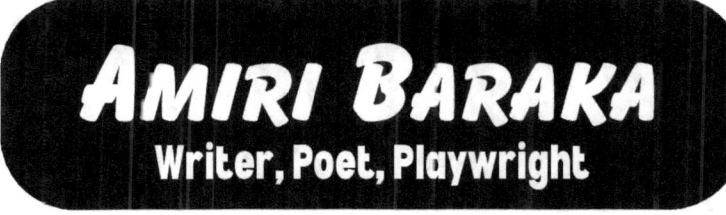

AMIRI BARAKA
Writer, Poet, Playwright

21

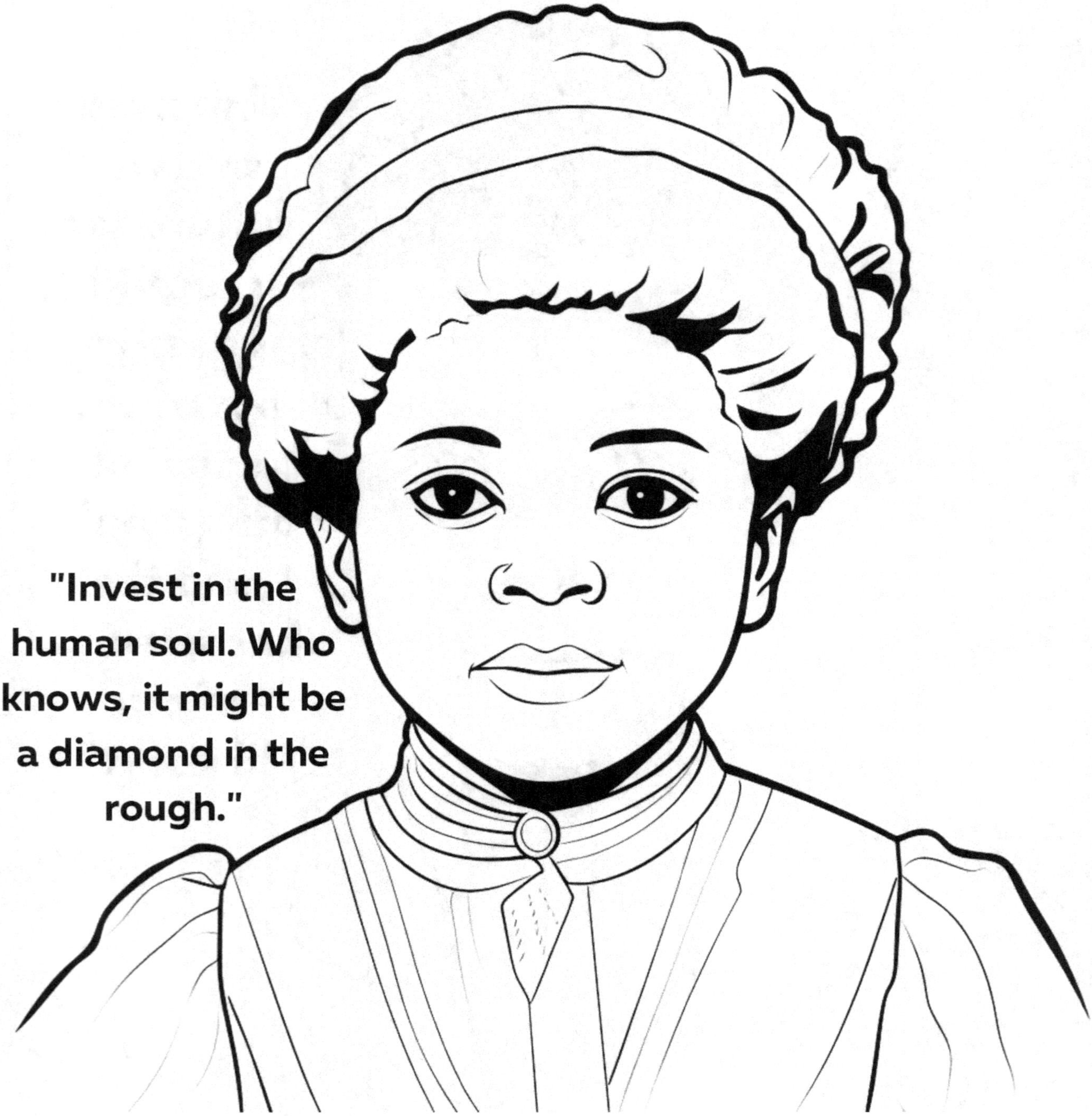

"Invest in the human soul. Who knows, it might be a diamond in the rough."

Mary McLeod Bethune (July 10, 1875 - May 18, 1955) was an educator, civil rights leader, and government advisor. She founded the Daytona Educational and Industrial Training School for Negro Girls, which later became Bethune-Cookman University. Bethune also served as an advisor to several U.S. presidents, advocating for racial and gender equality, economic opportunities, and educational reforms. Her leadership and activism helped expand educational opportunities for African Americans and laid the foundation for future advancements in civil rights

22

MARY McLEOD BETHUNE
Educator, Civil Rights Leader, Government Advisor

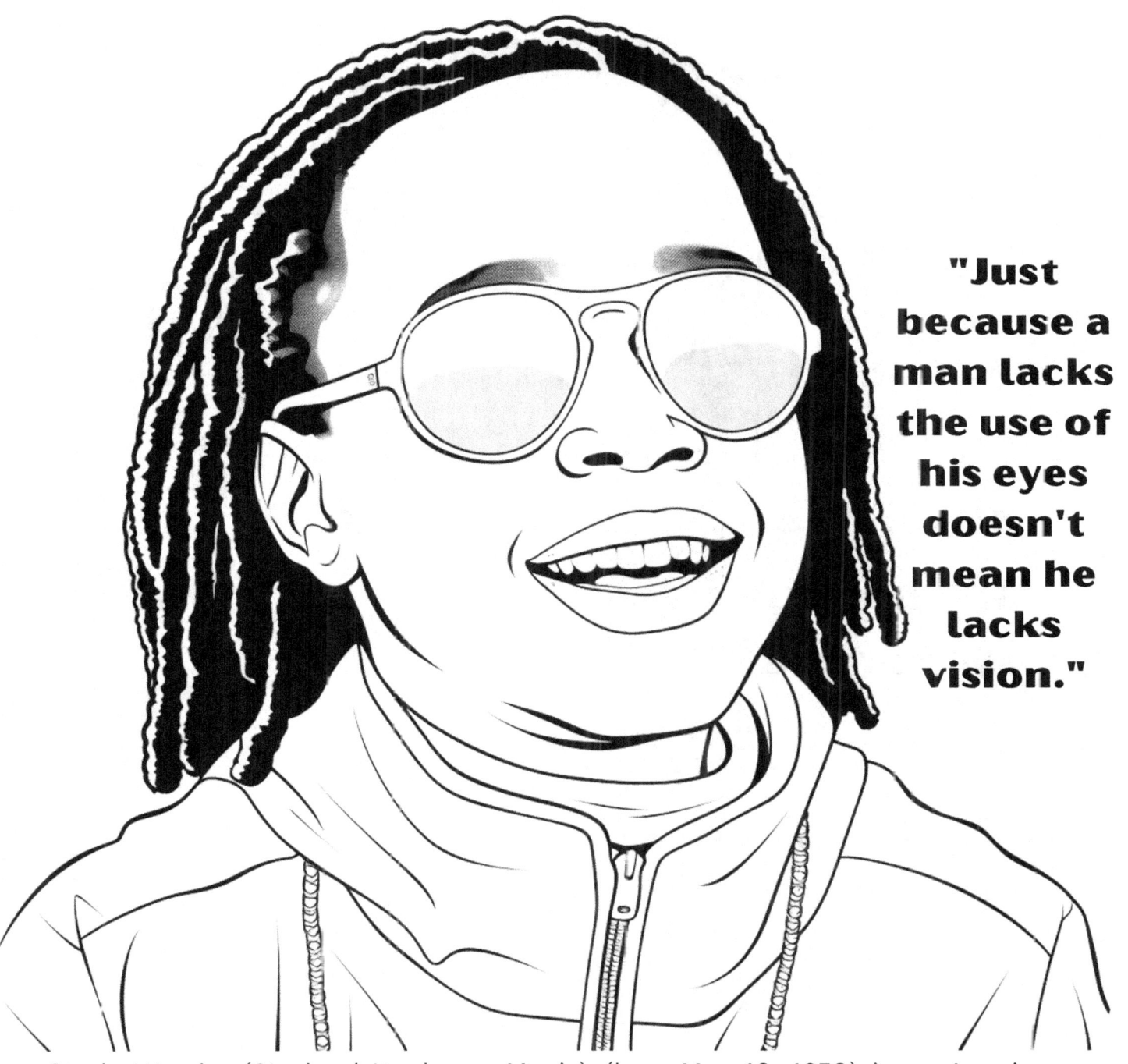

"Just because a man lacks the use of his eyes doesn't mean he lacks vision."

Stevie Wonder (Stevland Hardaway Morris) (born May 13, 1950) is an American singer, songwriter, and multi-instrumentalist. Blind from infancy, Wonder is known for his exceptional talent and contributions to the fields of soul, R&B, and pop music. With a career spanning several decades, he has produced numerous chart-topping hits and won multiple Grammy Awards. Beyond his musical achievements, Wonder has been a strong advocate for social causes, including civil rights, disability rights, and awareness of global issues. His songs, such as "Superstition" and "Living for the City," have become anthems of resilience and social consciousness.

STEVIE WONDER
Singer, Songwriter, Multi-instrumentalist

23

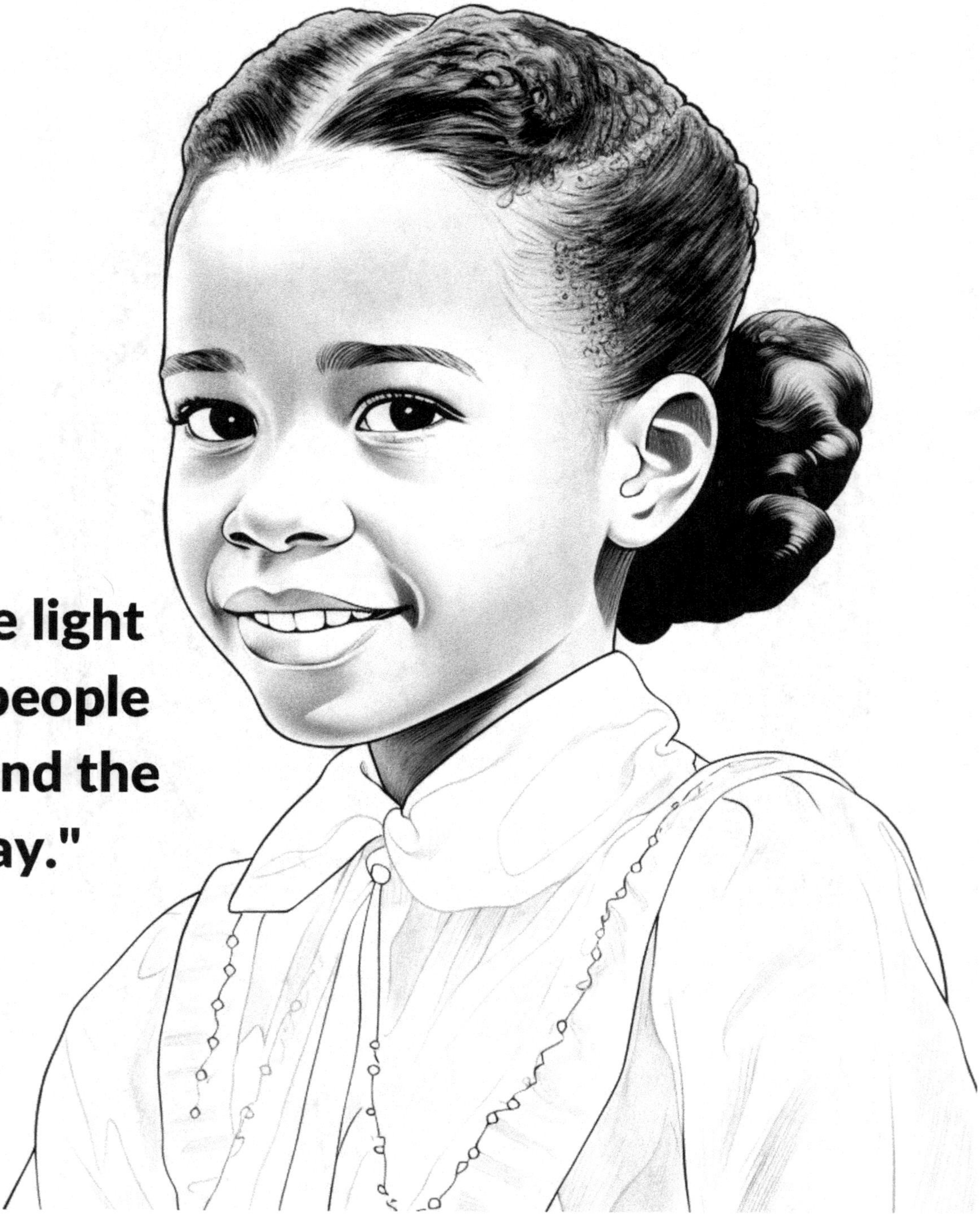

"Give light and people will find the way."

Ella Baker (December 13, 1903 – December 13, 1986) was a leading figure in the civil rights movement and a skilled organizer and strategist. She played a pivotal role in numerous civil rights organizations, including the NAACP and the Southern Christian Leadership Conference (SCLC). Baker was a strong proponent of grassroots organizing and empowering local communities. She worked tirelessly to mobilize and empower ordinary people, particularly young activists, to fight for their rights and challenge systemic racism. Baker's leadership and commitment to democratic participation continue to influence social justice movements today.

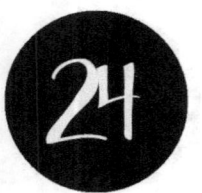

ELLA BAKER
Civil Rights Leader, Organizer, Strategist

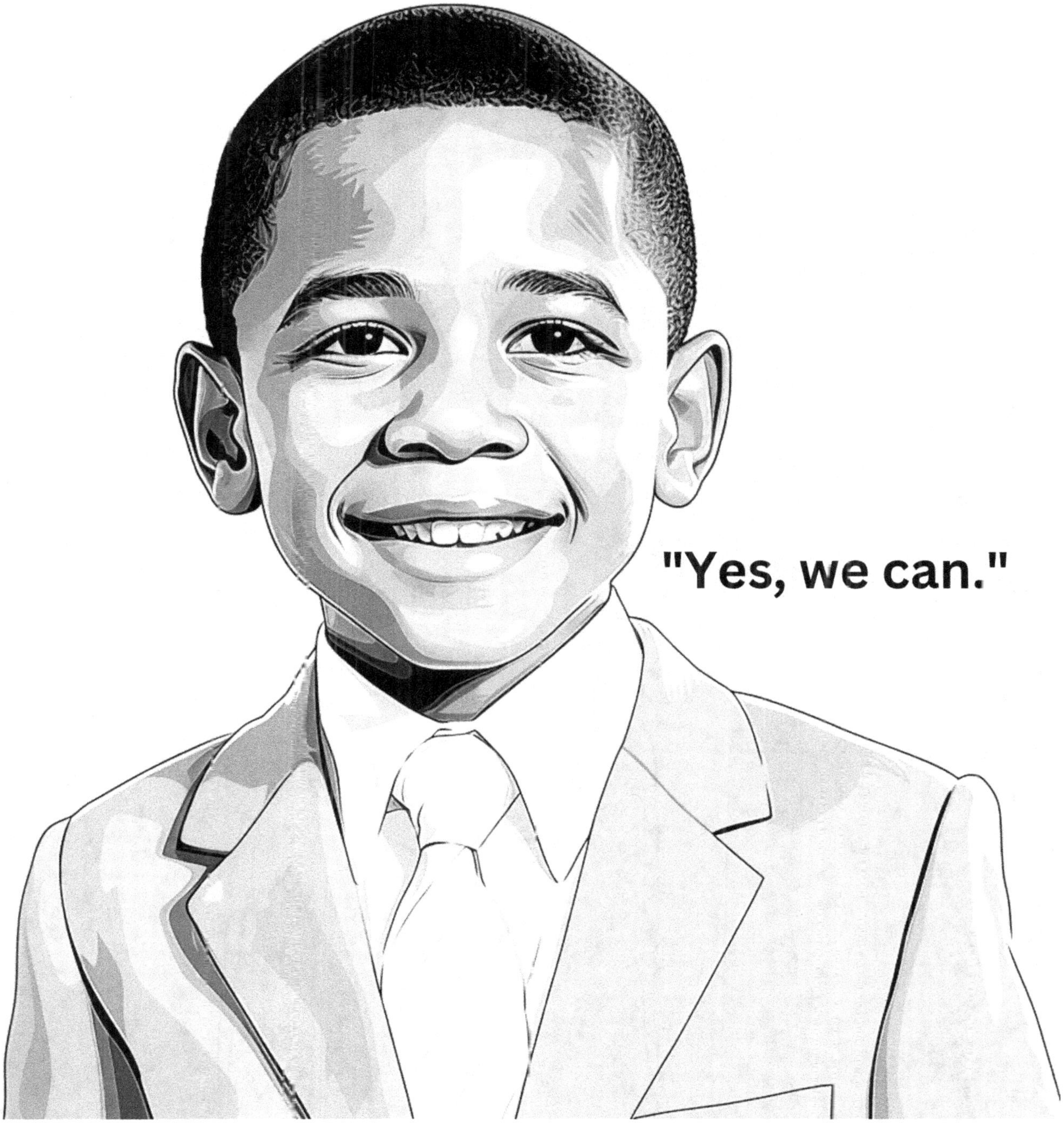

"Yes, we can."

Barack Obama (born August 4, 1961) is an American politician and the 44th President of the United States. He made history as the first African American to hold the presidency, serving from 2009 to 2017. Obama's presidency was marked by numerous accomplishments, including the passage of the Affordable Care Act, the Paris Agreement on climate change, and the economic recovery following the Great Recession. His leadership and message of hope and unity inspired millions of people around the world. Obama's historic presidency has had a lasting impact on American politics and representation.

BARACK OBAMA
44th President of the United States

25

"I am no longer accepting the things I cannot change. I am changing the things I cannot accept."

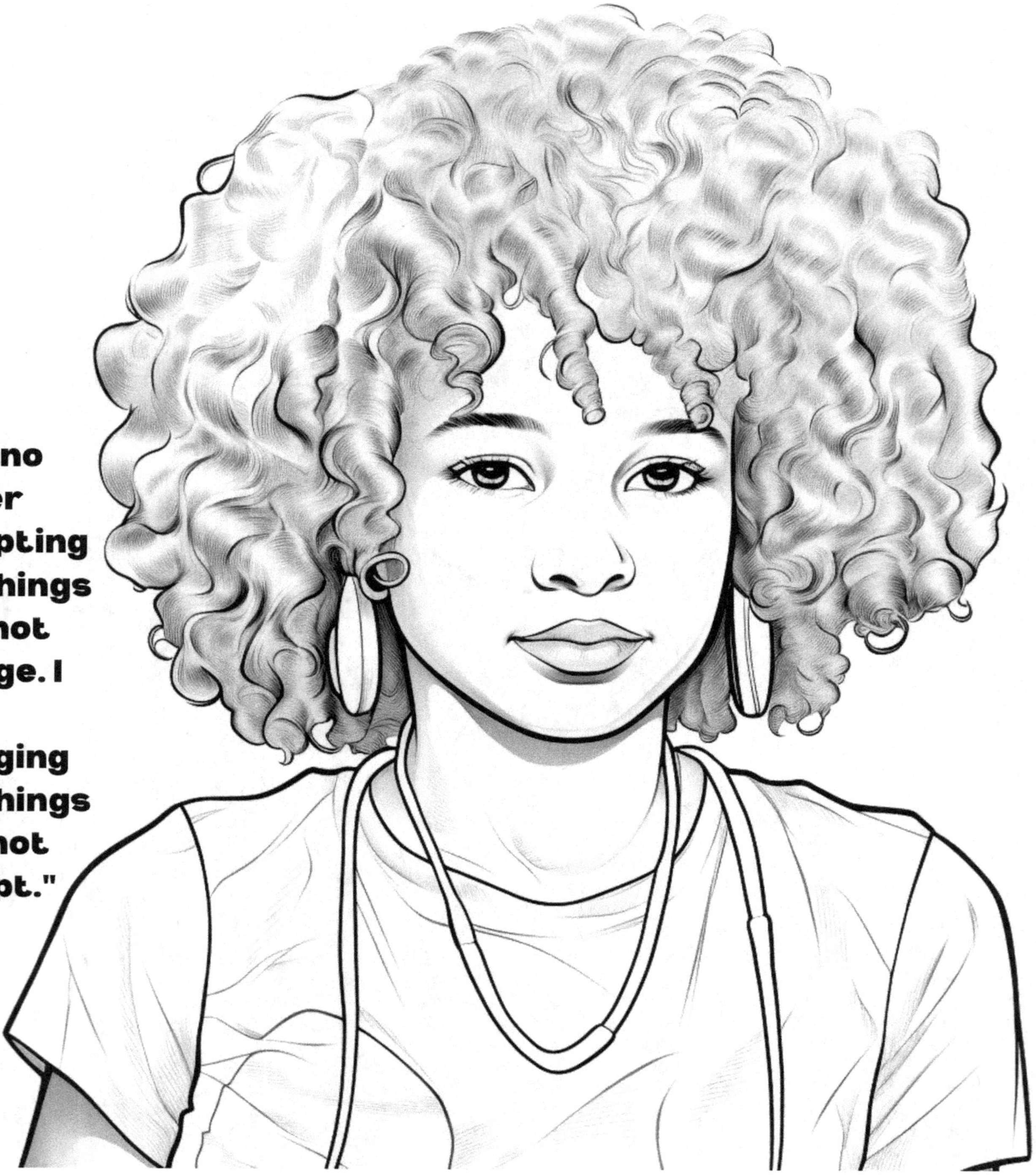

Angela Davis (born January 26, 1944) is an activist, scholar, and author who emerged as a prominent figure in the Black Power and communist movements of the 1960s and 1970s. Davis's work focuses on issues of racial and gender equality, prison abolition, and socialist theory. She has been an outspoken advocate for the rights of marginalized communities and has fought against systemic oppression. Davis's activism and writings continue to inspire generations of activists and scholars.

26

ANGELA DAVIS
Activist, Scholar, Author

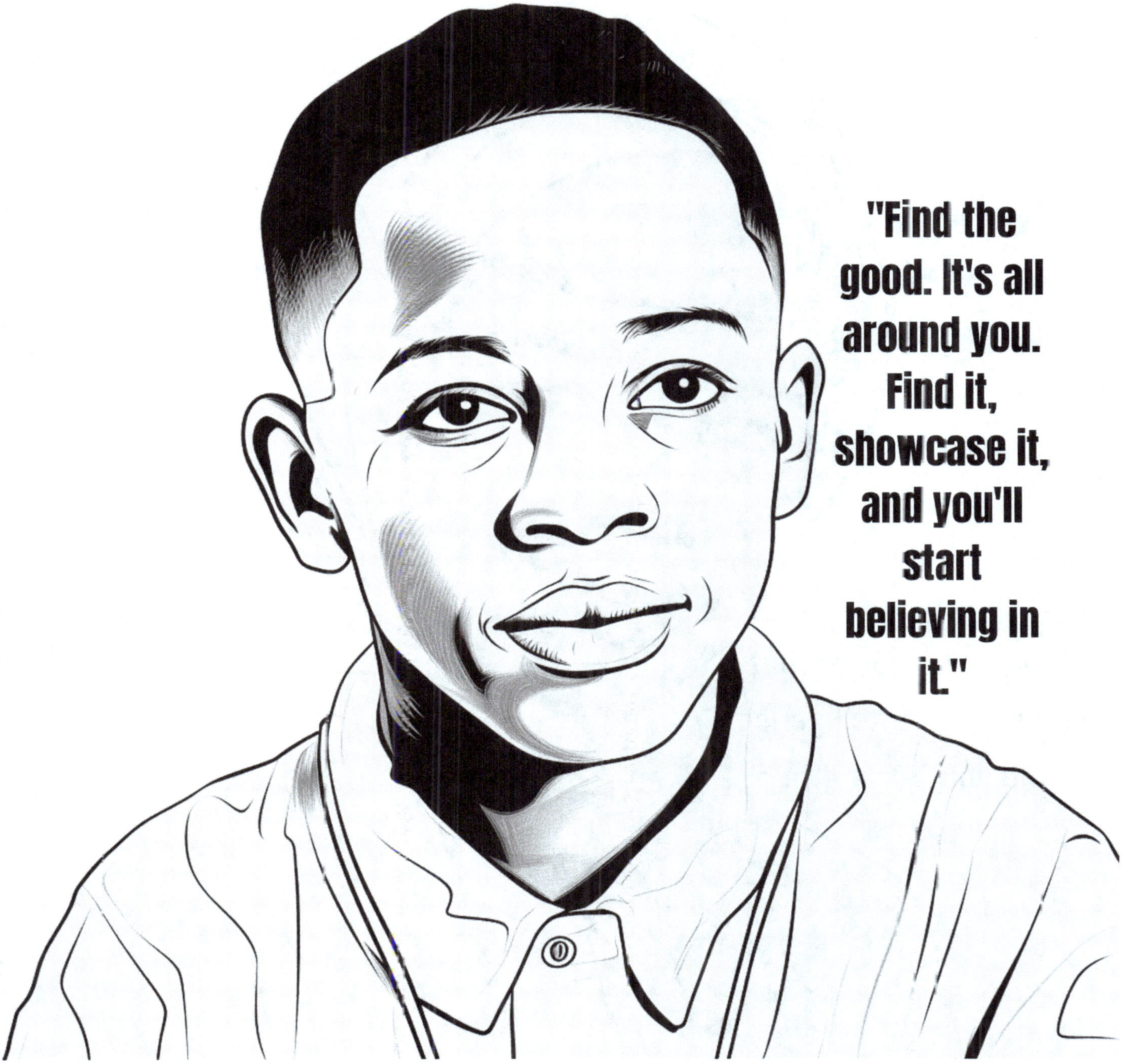

"Find the good. It's all around you. Find it, showcase it, and you'll start believing in it."

Jesse Owens (James Cleveland Owens) (September 12, 1913 – March 31, 1980) was a track and field athlete who achieved international acclaim during the 1936 Olympic Games in Berlin, Germany. Despite the racial discrimination prevalent at the time, Owens won four gold medals, setting world records in the process. His victories, including his historic long jump performance, shattered the myth of Aryan racial superiority promoted by the Nazi regime. Owens' achievements not only made him a sports legend but also served as a powerful symbol of Black excellence and resistance against racism.

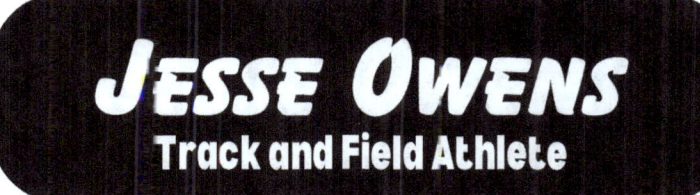

JESSE OWENS
Track and Field Athlete

27

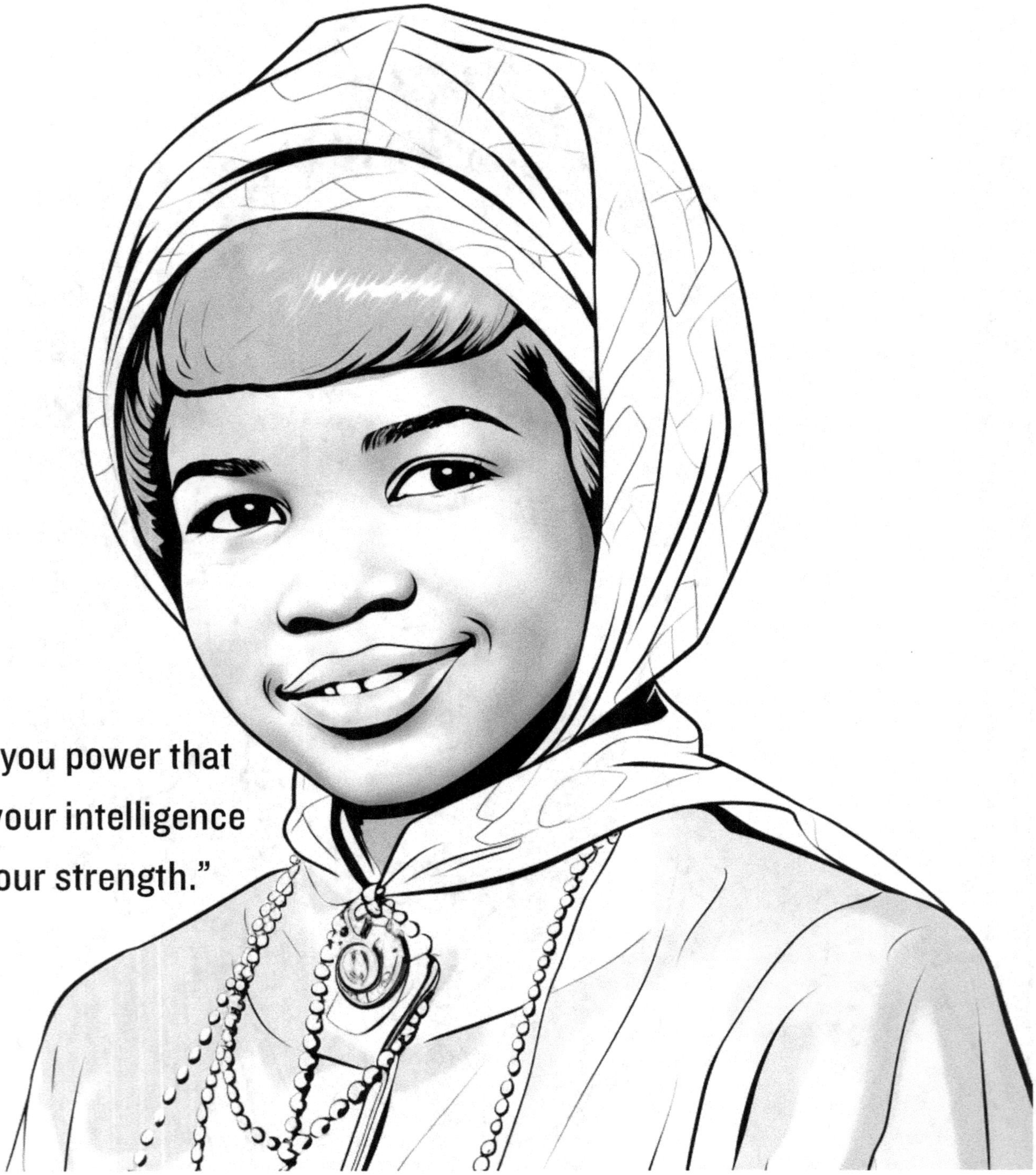

"I wish you power that equals your intelligence and your strength."

Betty Shabazz (Betty Dean Sanders) (May 28, 1934 – June 23, 1997) was an educator, civil rights advocate, and the widow of Malcolm X. After her husband's assassination in 1965, Shabazz dedicated herself to raising their six daughters and continuing their work for social justice. She earned a doctoral degree in education and became a college administrator, focusing on supporting minority students. Shabazz also played a significant role in preserving Malcolm X's legacy and promoting his teachings. Throughout her life, she emphasized the importance of education, community engagement, and empowerment.

28

BETTY SHABAZZ
Educator, Civil Rights Advocate

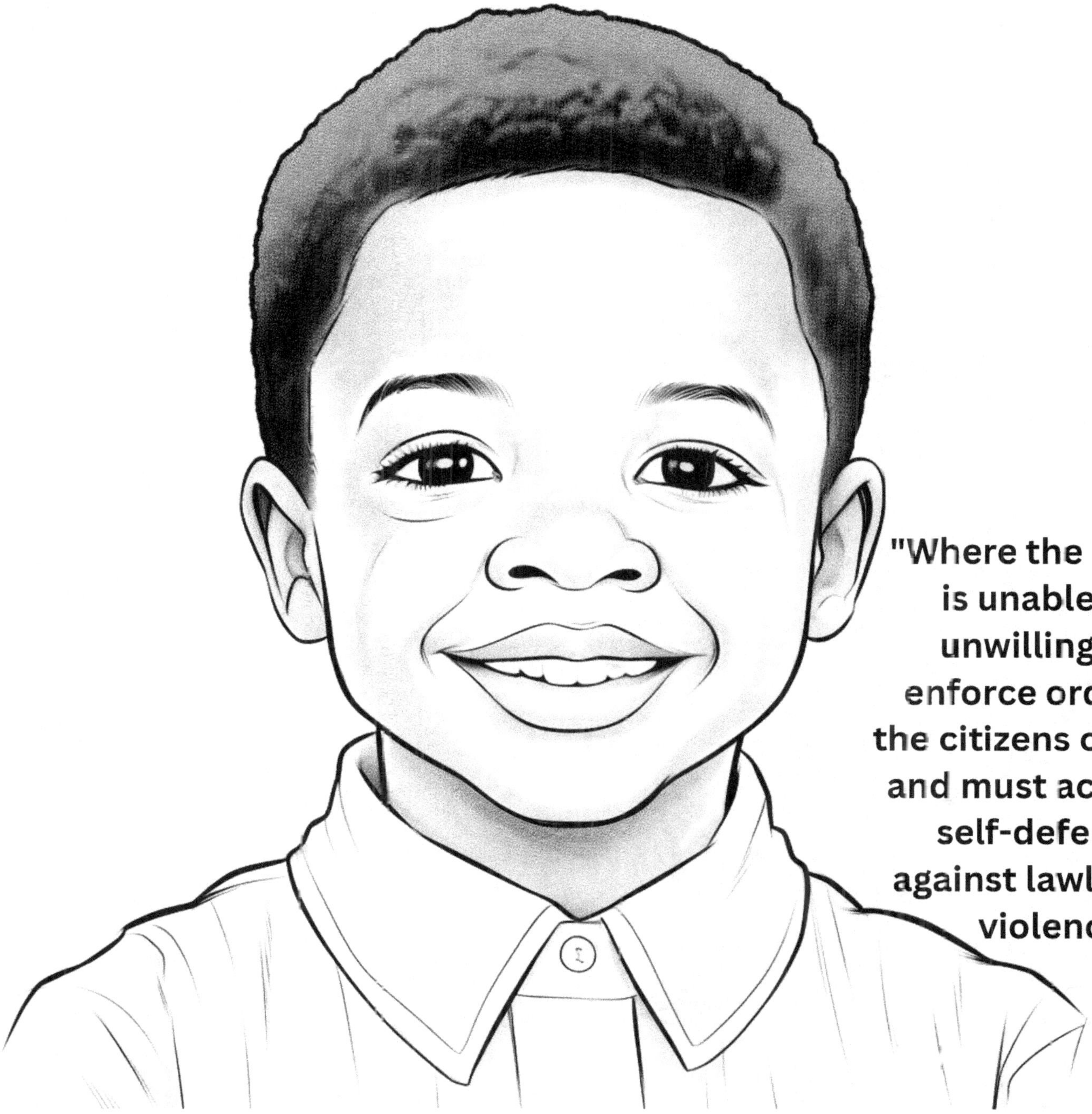

> "Where the law is unable, or unwilling, to enforce order, the citizens can, and must act in self-defense against lawless violence."

Robert F. Williams (February 26, 1925 – October 15, 1996) was a civil rights leader and advocate for armed self-defense in the face of racial violence. As the president of the Monroe, North Carolina, chapter of the NAACP, Williams organized African Americans to protect themselves and their communities during the turbulent era of Jim Crow segregation. He is best known for his book, "Negroes with Guns" (1962), which argued for self-defense and sparked debate within the civil rights movement. Williams' courageous efforts to challenge white supremacy and fight for equality laid the foundation for future activism.

ROBERT F. WILLIAMS
Civil Rights Leader, Author

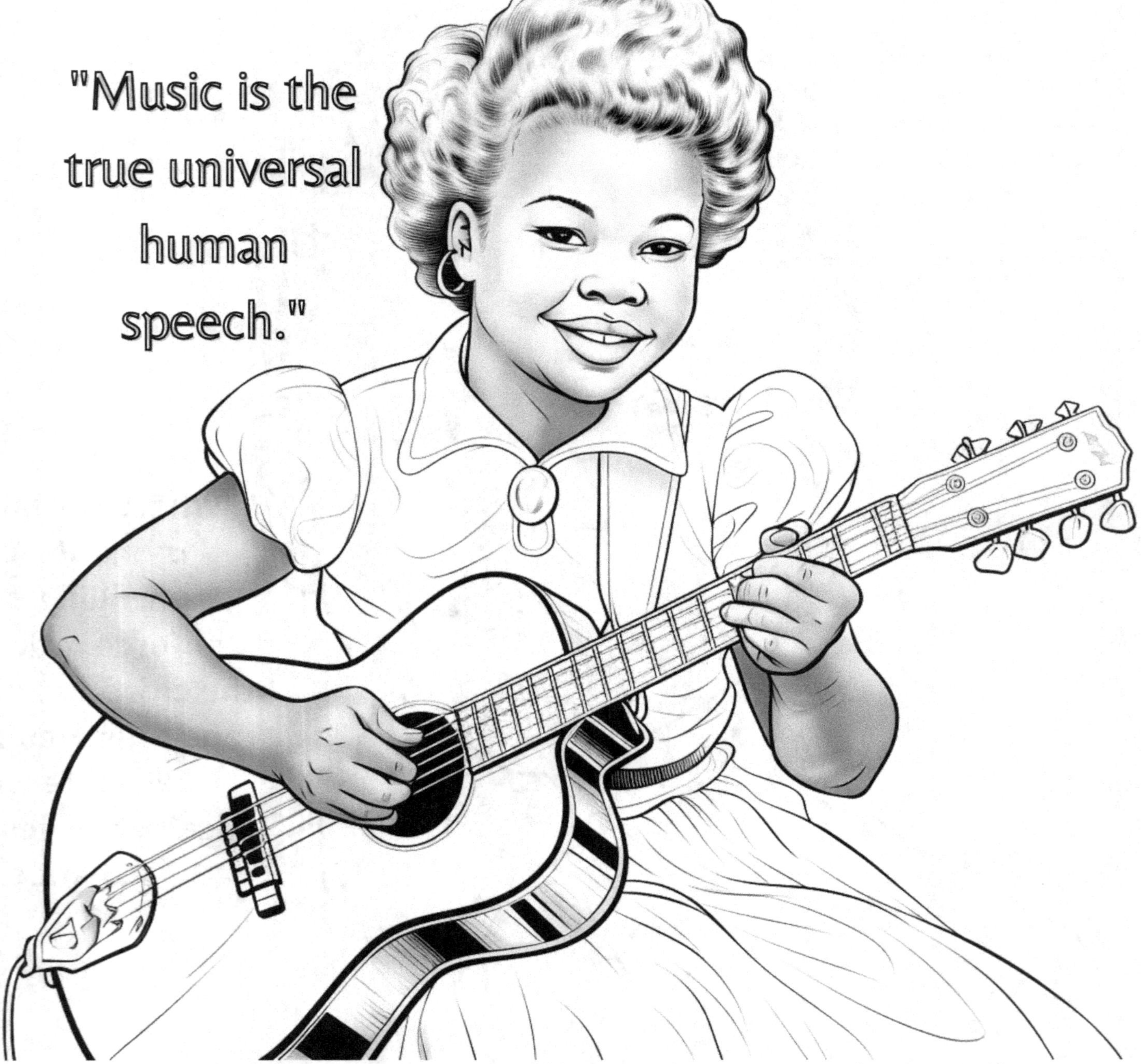

"Music is the true universal human speech."

Rosetta Tharpe (Sister Rosetta Tharpe) (March 20, 1915 – October 9, 1973) was a pioneering singer, songwriter, and guitarist who is often referred to as the "Godmother of Rock and Roll." Her unique blend of gospel, blues, and early rock and roll influenced numerous musicians and helped shape the sound of popular music. Tharpe's powerful vocals and energetic guitar playing captivated audiences, and she became a sensation during the 1930s and 1940s. Her music broke down barriers and crossed racial and genre boundaries, leaving a lasting impact on the music industry.

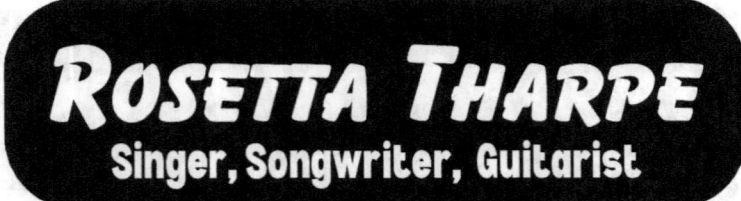

ROSETTA THARPE
Singer, Songwriter, Guitarist

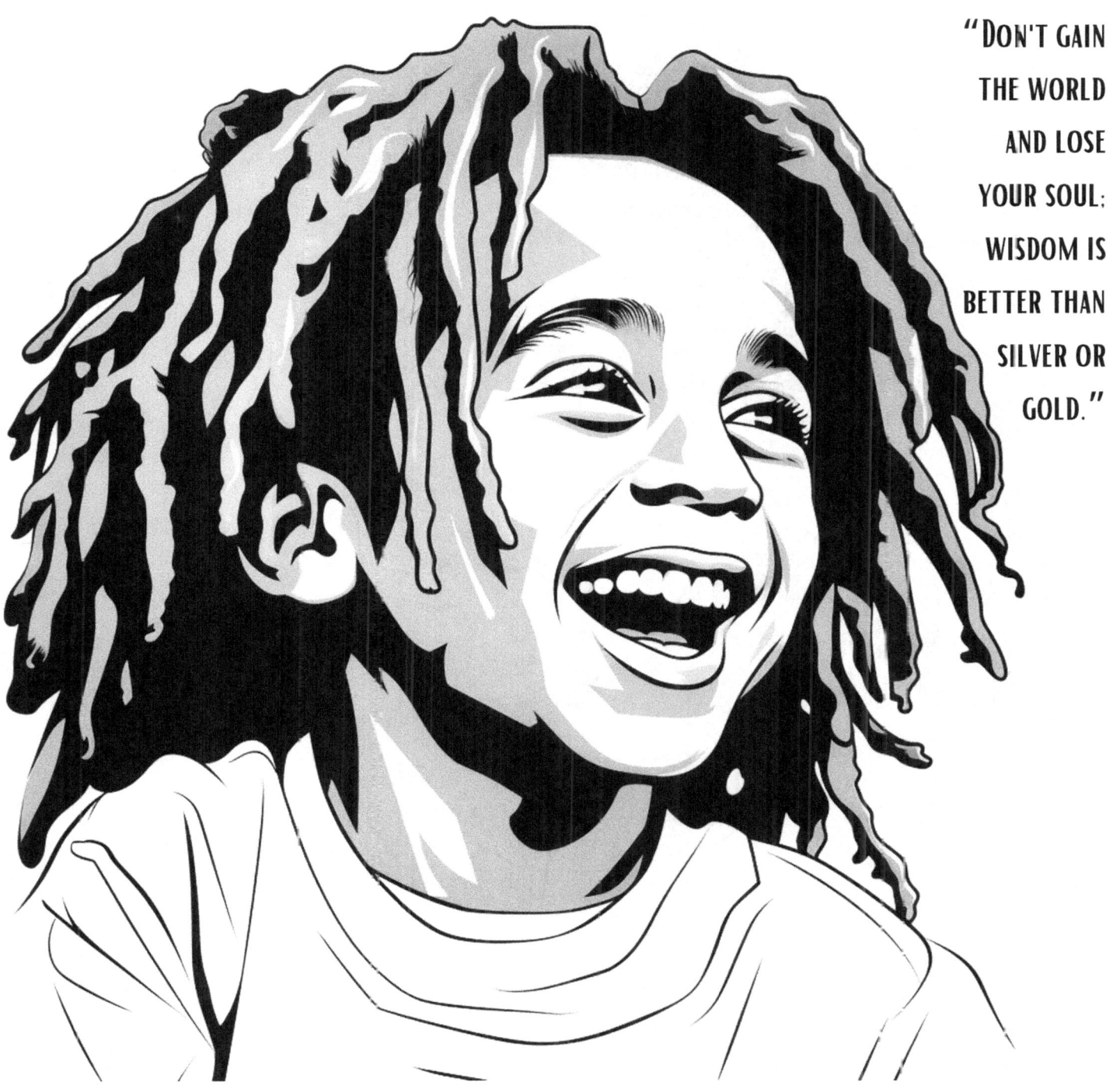

"DON'T GAIN THE WORLD AND LOSE YOUR SOUL; WISDOM IS BETTER THAN SILVER OR GOLD."

Bob Marley (Robert Nesta Marley) (February 6, 1945 – May 11, 1981) was a Jamaican musician, singer, and songwriter, and one of the most influential figures in reggae music. His music, characterized by its messages of love, unity, and social justice, helped popularize reggae music globally. Marley's iconic songs, including "One Love" and "Redemption Song," continue to inspire people around the world and serve as anthems for peace and equality. Marley's legacy as a musician and activist has had a profound and enduring impact on popular culture.

BOB MARLEY
Musician, Singer, Songwriter

31

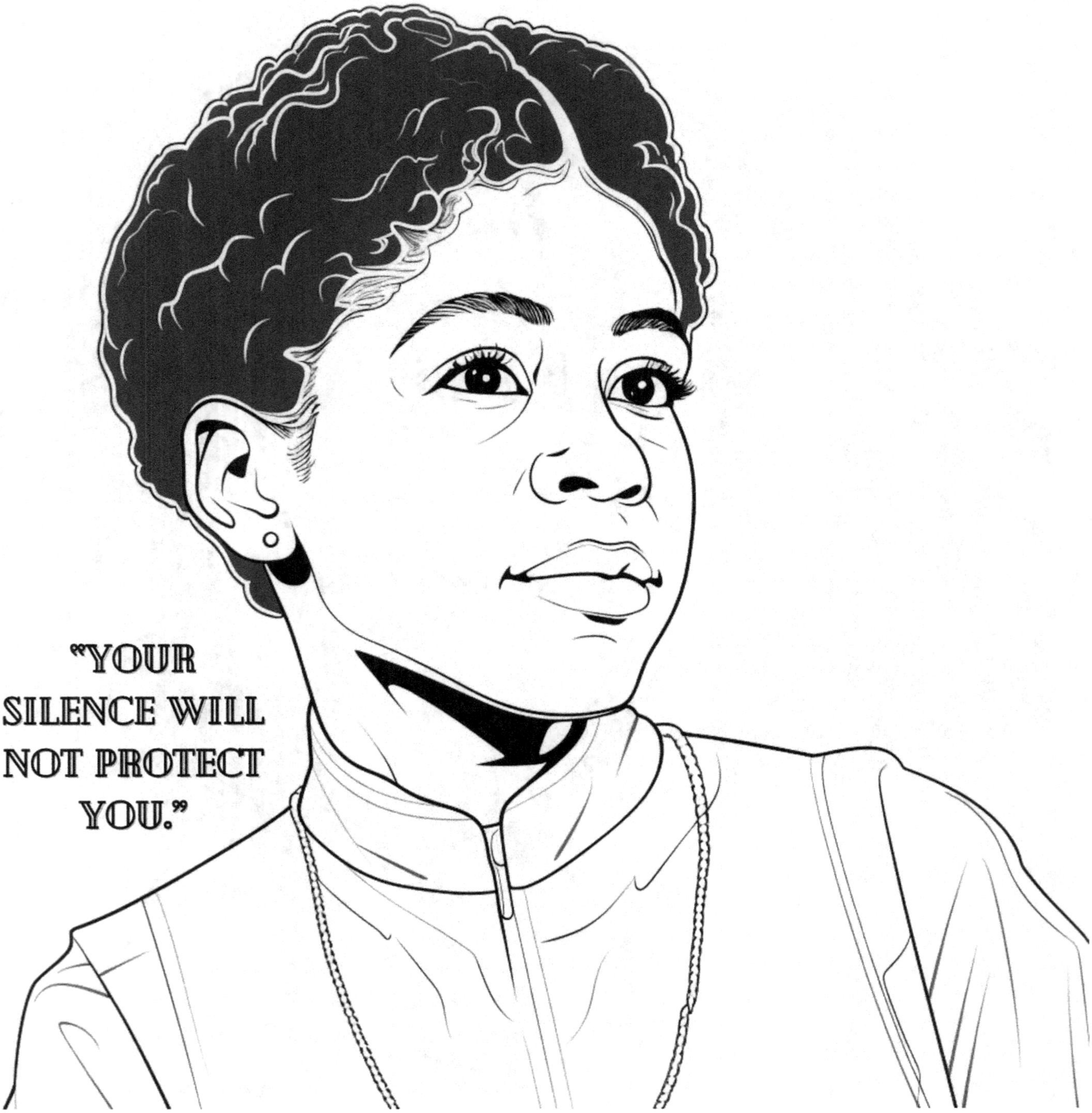

"YOUR SILENCE WILL NOT PROTECT YOU."

Audre Lorde (February 18, 1934 – November 17, 1992) was a Black feminist writer, poet, and civil rights activist. Lorde's writings, such as "The Cancer Journals" (1980) and "Zami: A New Spelling of My Name" (1982), explored intersecting identities, including race, gender, and sexuality. She advocated for the empowerment of marginalized communities and used her work to address social and political issues, including racism, homophobia, and sexism. Lorde's poetry and essays continue to be influential in feminist and queer literature.

32

AUDRE LORDE
Feminist Writer, Poet, Civil Rights Activist

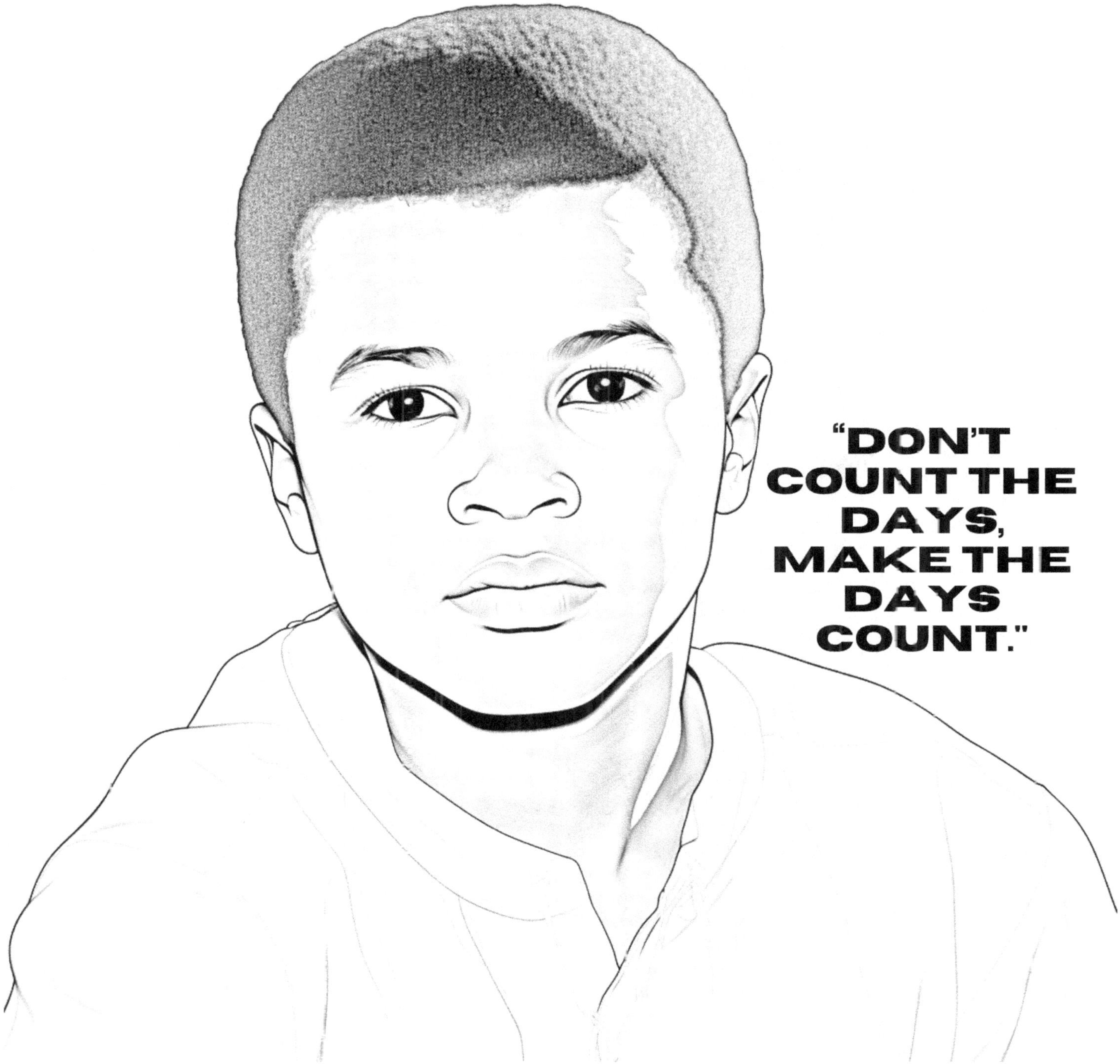

"DON'T COUNT THE DAYS, MAKE THE DAYS COUNT."

Muhammad Ali (Cassius Clay) (January 17, 1942 – June 3, 2016) was a professional boxer and one of the most iconic sports figures of the 20th century. Known for his unmatched skills in the ring, Ali became a three-time world heavyweight champion. Beyond boxing, Ali was a powerful advocate for racial equality, religious freedom, and social justice. He famously refused to be drafted into the Vietnam War, citing his religious and moral beliefs. Ali's charisma, activism, and unapologetic self-expression made him an influential figure both inside and outside the boxing ring.

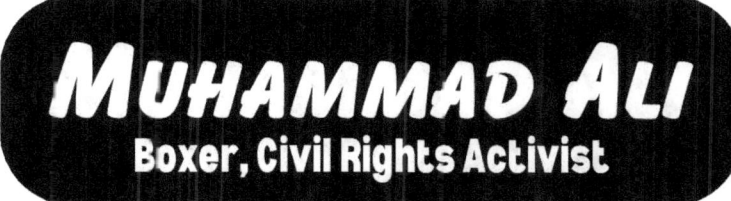

MUHAMMAD ALI
Boxer, Civil Rights Activist

33

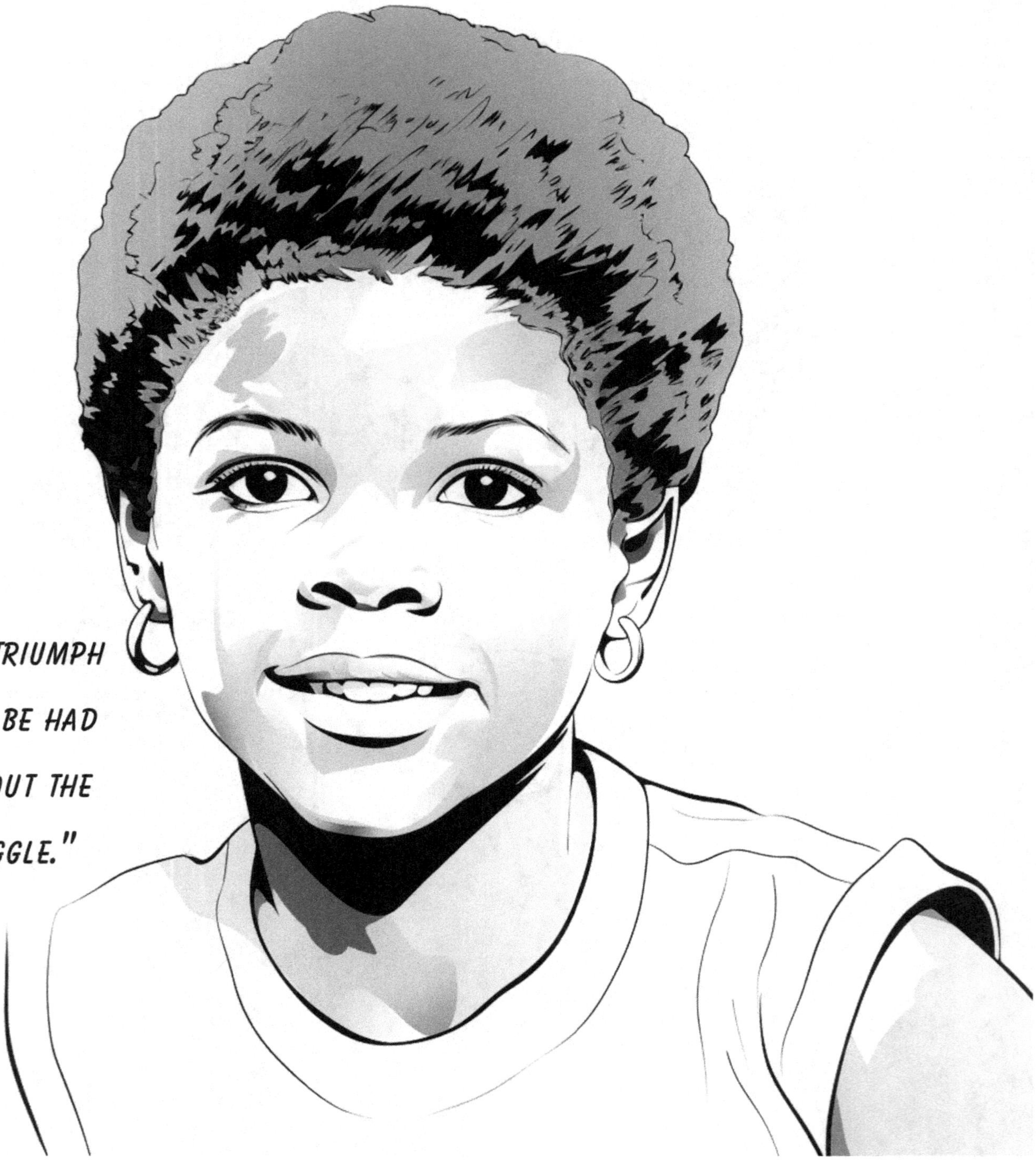

"The triumph can't be had without the struggle."

Wilma Rudolph (June 23, 1940 – November 12, 1994) was a track and field athlete who overcame significant physical challenges to become one of the most successful sprinters in history. Rudolph, who contracted polio as a child, went on to win three gold medals at the 1960 Olympic Games, becoming the first American woman to achieve such a feat. Her accomplishments not only made her a sporting legend but also inspired countless individuals with disabilities and helped break down racial barriers in the world of athletics.

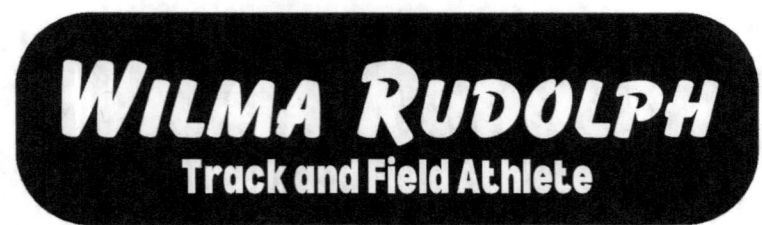

WILMA RUDOLPH
Track and Field Athlete

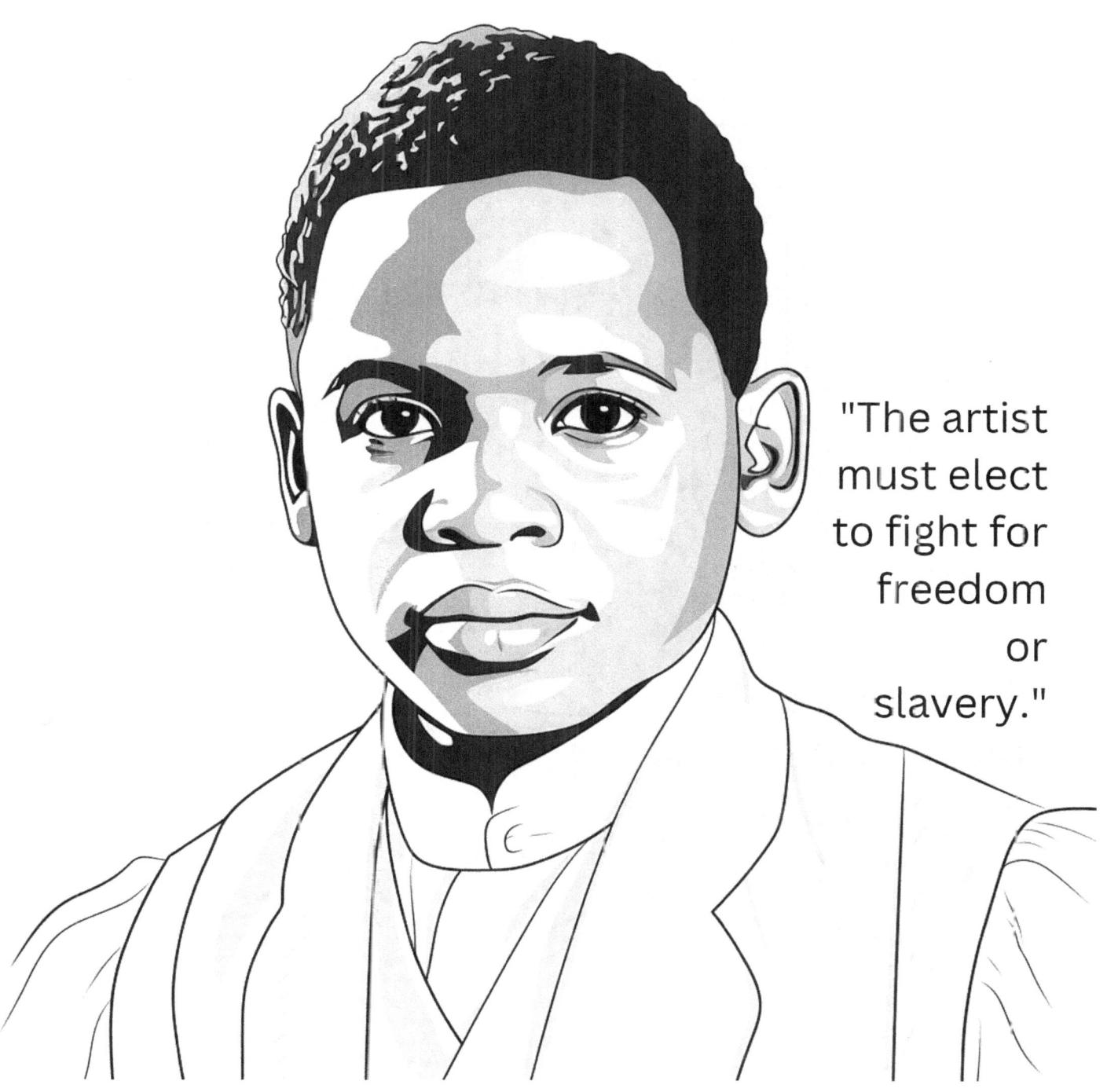

"The artist must elect to fight for freedom or slavery."

Paul Robeson (April 9, 1898 - January 23, 1976) was a singer, actor, athlete, and civil rights activist. Robeson's powerful bass-baritone voice and commanding stage presence made him a celebrated performer on both Broadway and the opera stage. He used his platform to advocate for civil rights, labor rights, and global peace. Robeson's activism and outspokenness on issues of racial equality and social justice led to his blacklisting during the McCarthy era, but he continued to fight for justice and equality until the end of his life.

PAUL ROBESON
Singer, Actor, Athlete, Civil Rights Activist

35

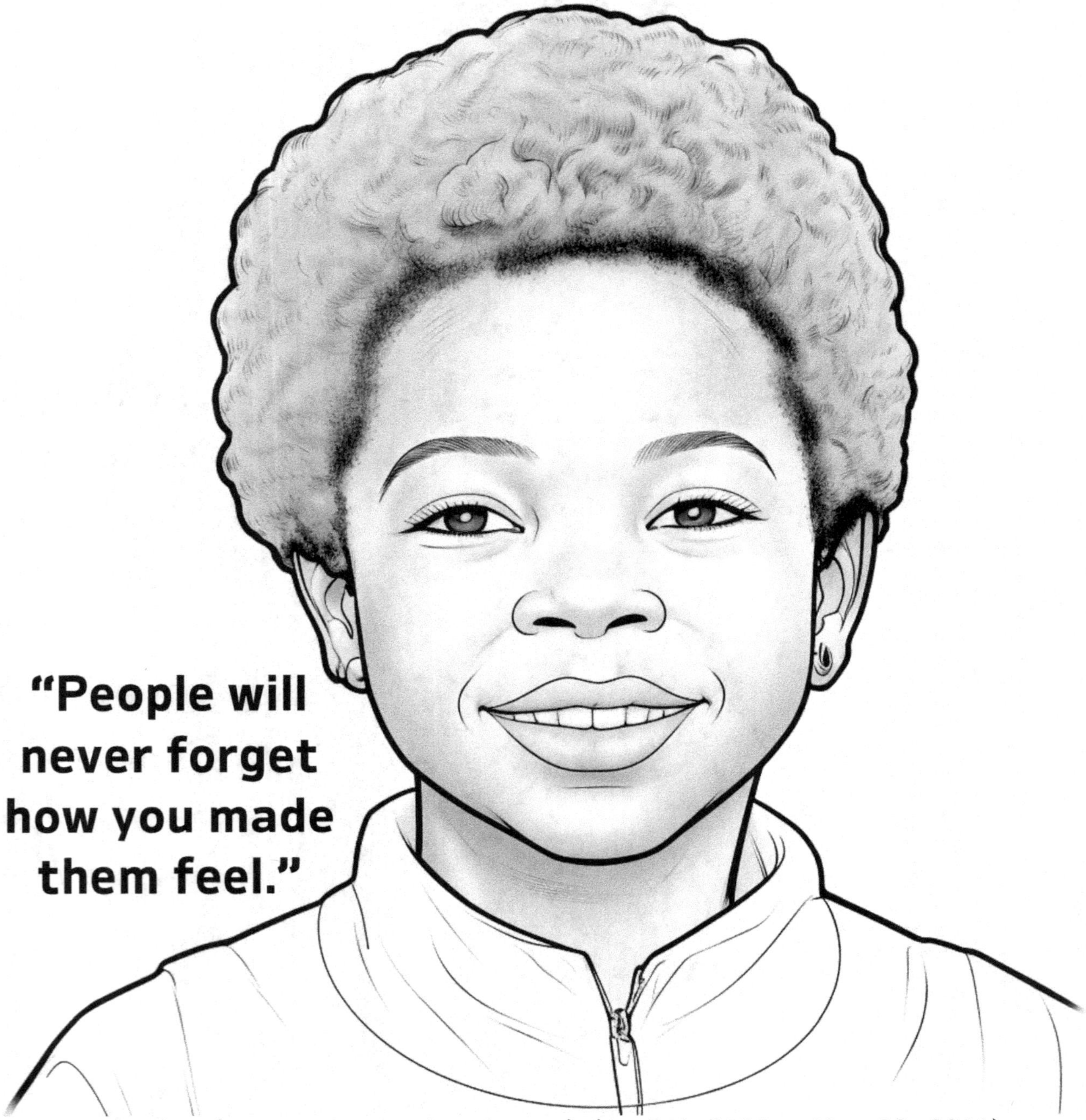

"People will never forget how you made them feel."

Maya Angelou (Marguerite Annie Johnson) (April 4, 1928 – May 28, 2014) was an acclaimed poet, memoirist, and civil rights activist. Her memoir, "I Know Why the Caged Bird Sings" (1969), gained widespread acclaim for its honest portrayal of her experiences growing up in the racially segregated South. Angelou's eloquent poetry and powerful storytelling brought attention to the African-American experience, gender inequality, and social justice issues. Her contributions to literature and her advocacy for civil rights earned her numerous awards, including the Presidential Medal of Freedom.

36

MAYA ANGELOU
Poet, Memoirist, Civil Rights Activist

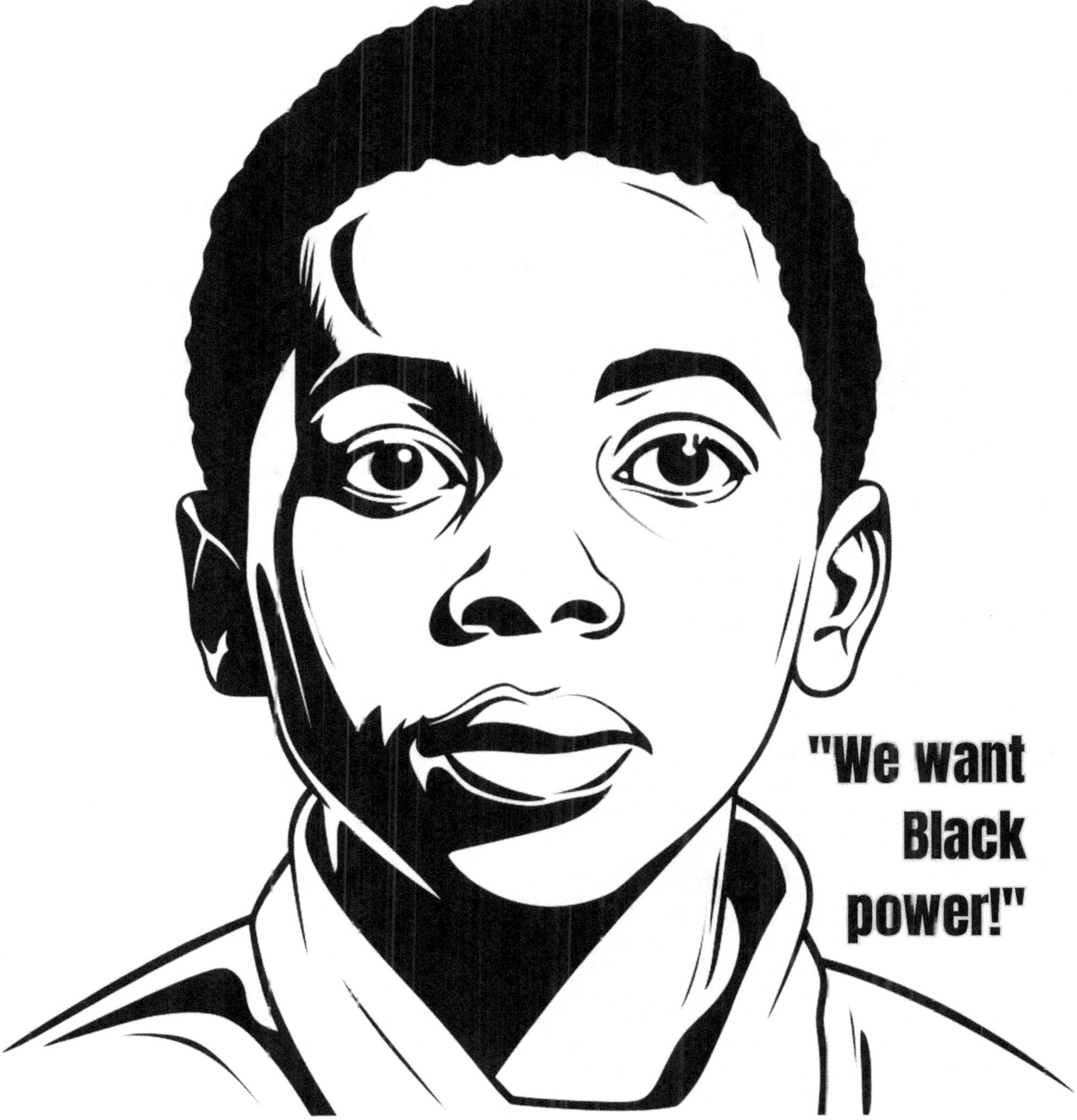

"We want Black power!"

Stokely Carmichael (Kwame Ture) (June 29, 1941 – November 15, 1998), later known as Kwame Ture, was a prominent civil rights activist and leader of the Black Power movement. Carmichael's passionate speeches and charismatic leadership style helped galvanize the fight against racial injustice and systemic oppression. He popularized the phrase "Black Power" and advocated for self-determination, community empowerment, and political resistance. Carmichael's influential role in the civil rights movement left a lasting impact on the struggle for Black liberation in the United States.

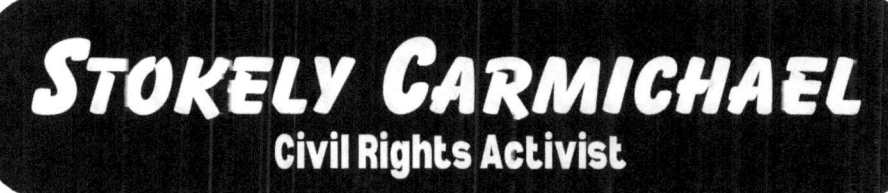

STOKELY CARMICHAEL
Civil Rights Activist

37

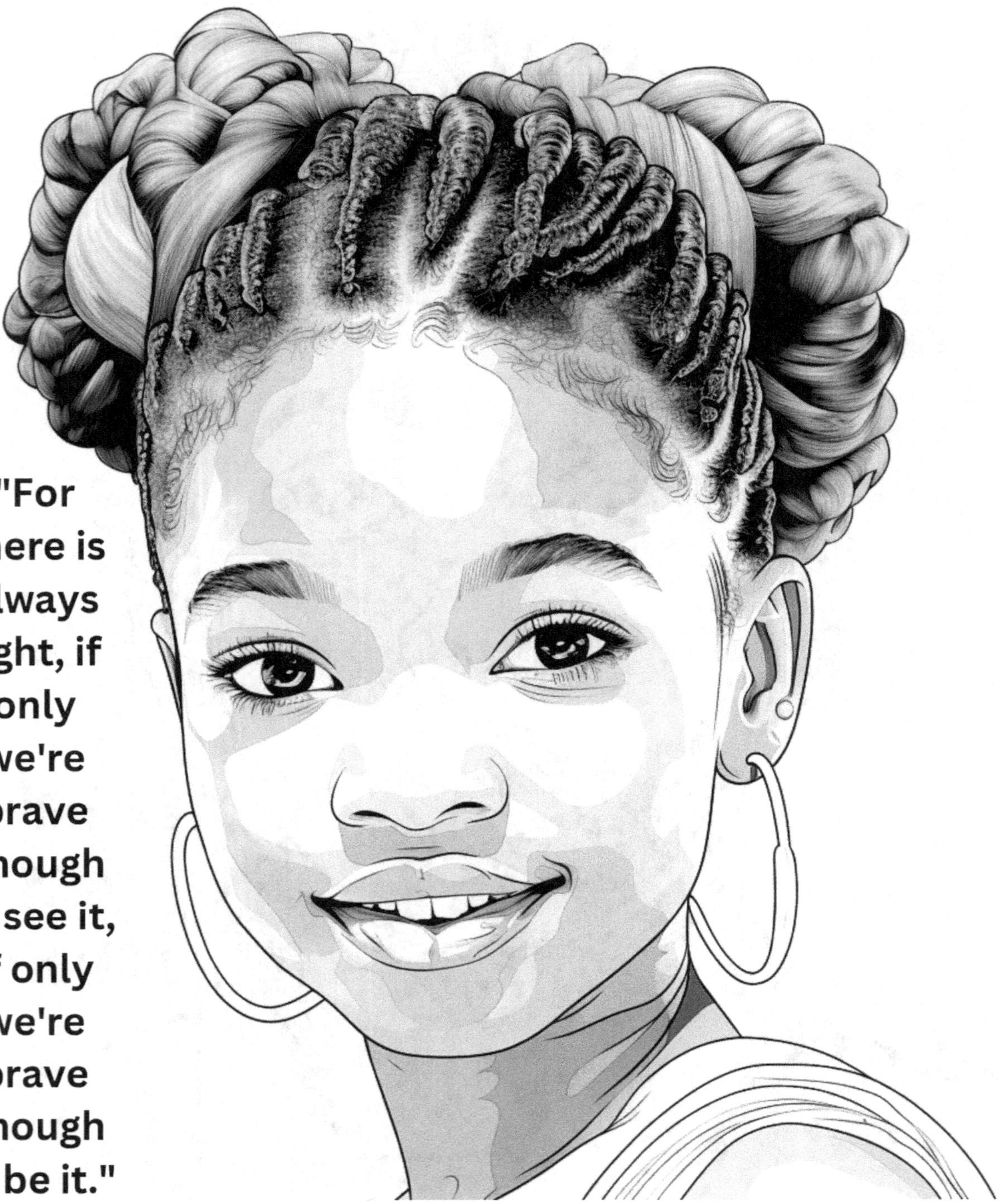

"For there is always light, if only we're brave enough to see it, if only we're brave enough to be it."

Amanda Gorman (born March 7, 1998) is an American poet and activist. She gained widespread acclaim for her powerful poem, "The Hill We Climb," which she recited at the inauguration of President Joe Biden in 2021. Gorman became the youngest poet in U.S. history to deliver a poem at a presidential inauguration. Her poetry explores themes of race, feminism, and the African-American experience, and she uses her words to inspire and advocate for positive social change. Gorman's eloquence and talent have made her a prominent voice for a new generation.

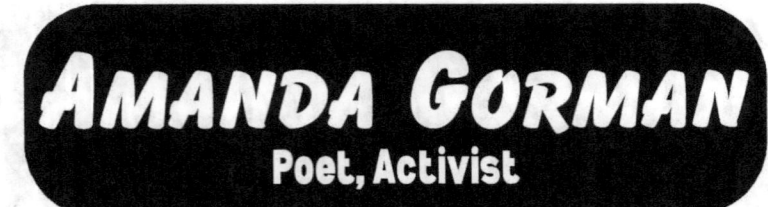

AMANDA GORMAN
Poet, Activist

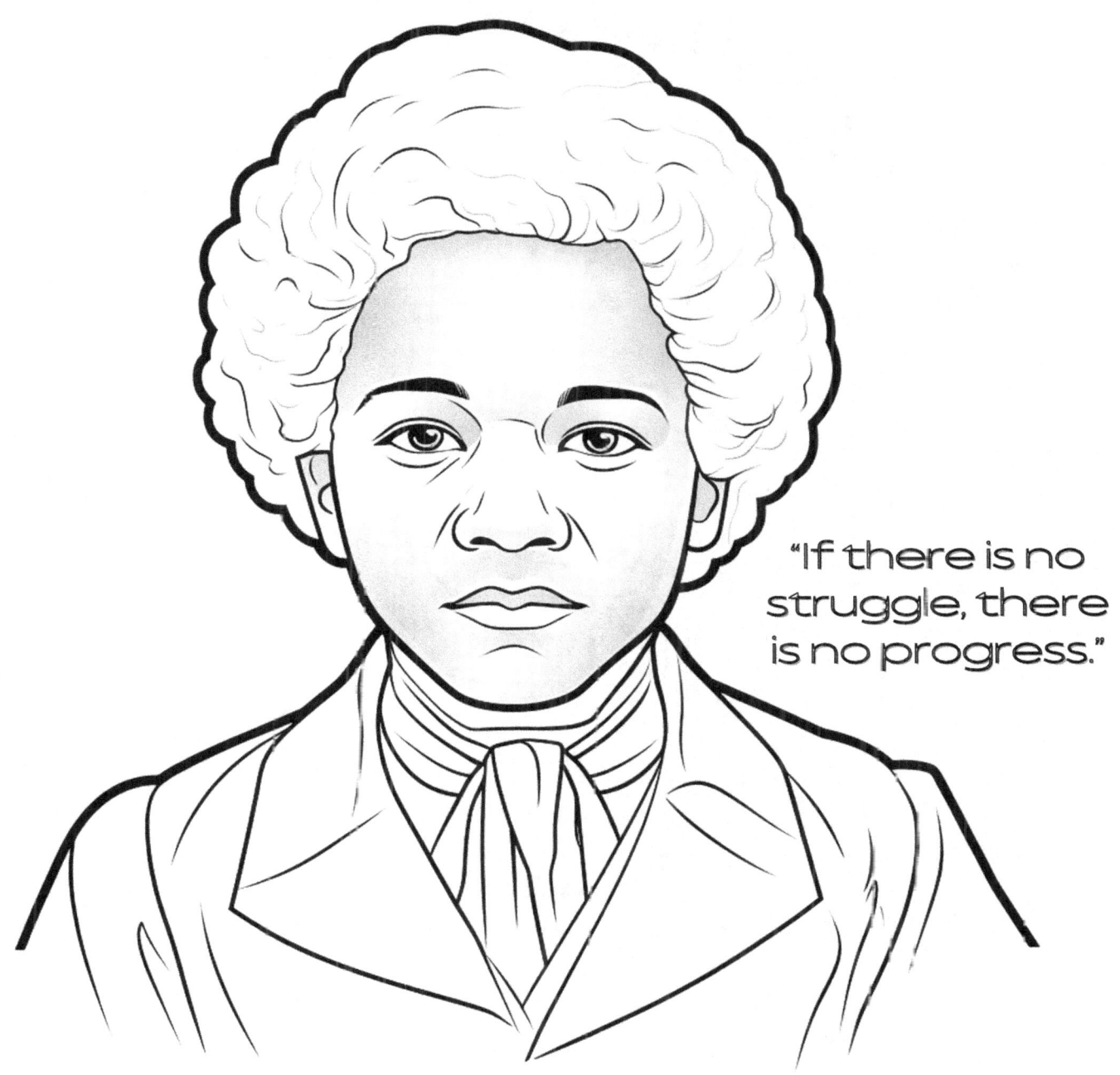

"If there is no struggle, there is no progress."

Frederick Douglass (c. February 1818 – February 20, 1895) was a social reformer, abolitionist, orator, writer, and statesman. Born into slavery, Douglass escaped to the North and became a prominent voice against slavery. His powerful autobiography, "Narrative of the Life of Frederick Douglass, an American Slave" (1845), exposed the harsh realities of slavery and helped galvanize the abolitionist movement. Douglass continued his advocacy for civil rights and equality, serving in various government positions and tirelessly fighting for the rights of African Americans.

FREDERICK DOUGLASS
Social Reformer, Abolitionist, Orator, Writer, Statesman

39

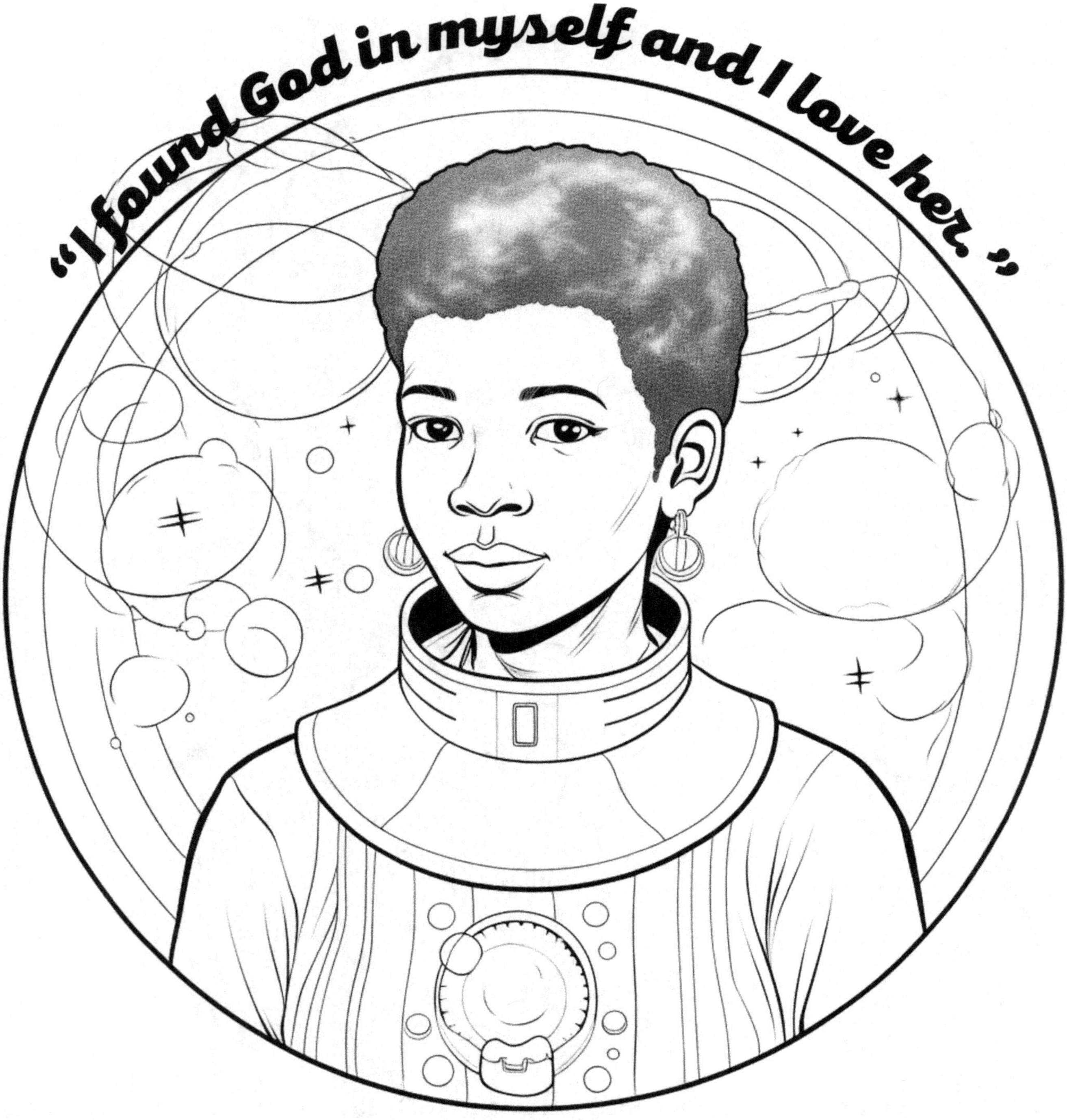

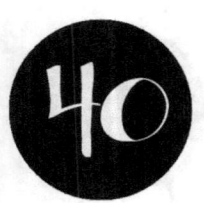

"I found God in myself and I love her."

Octavia Butler (June 22, 1947 - February 24, 2006) was a highly regarded science fiction writer. Her novels, such as "Kindred" (1979) and the "Parable" series (1993–1998), explored complex social and political issues through the lens of speculative fiction. Butler broke new ground as a Black female writer in a genre predominantly dominated by white male authors. Her insightful and thought-provoking works earned her numerous awards, including the prestigious MacArthur Fellowship, and solidified her legacy as a pioneer of Afrofuturism.

40

OCTAVIA BUTLER
Science Fiction Writer

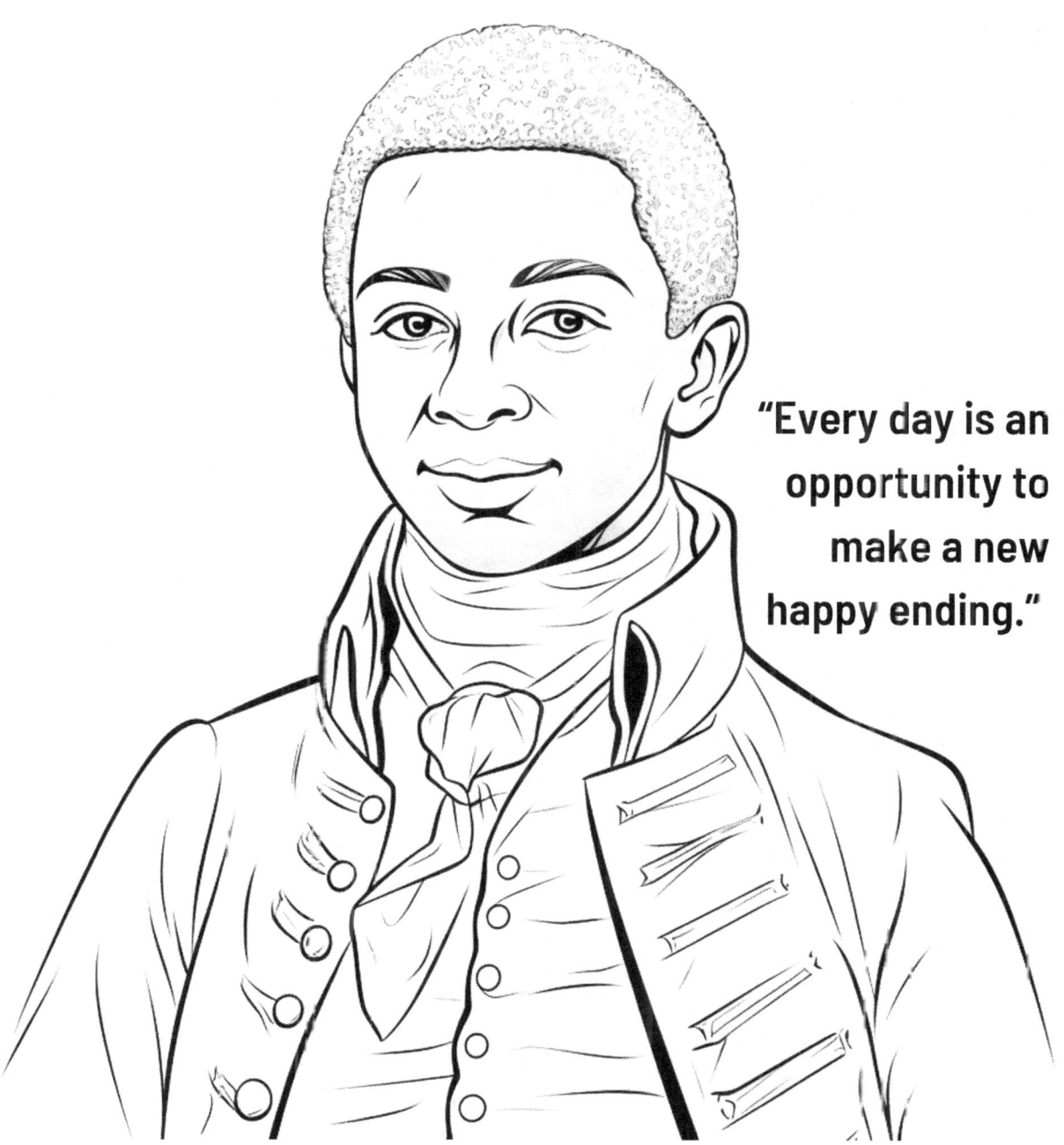

"Every day is an opportunity to make a new happy ending."

Benjamin Banneker (November 9, 1731 – October 9, 1806) was a self-taught mathematician, astronomer, and inventor. Despite being born into slavery, Banneker's intelligence and dedication to learning allowed him to excel in various scientific pursuits. He is best known for his construction of a wooden clock and his calculations to predict solar and lunar eclipses. Banneker's almanacs, which included his astronomical calculations and writings against slavery, brought him recognition as a respected figure in both scientific and social circles.

BENJAMIN BANNEKER
Mathematician, Astronomer, Inventor

41

"I freed a thousand slaves. I could have freed a thousand more if only they knew they were slaves."

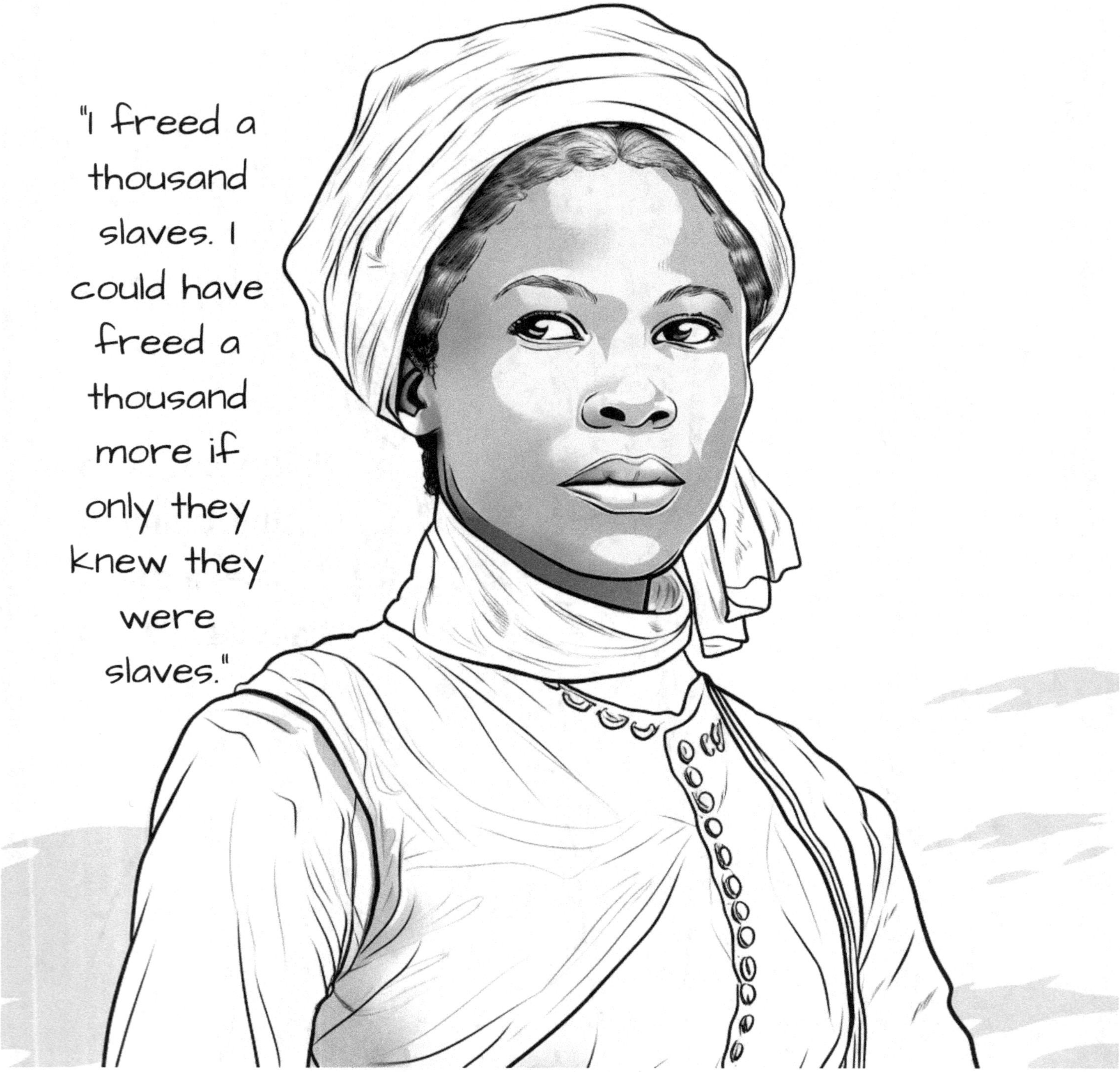

Harriet Tubman (c. 1820 – March 10, 1913) was an abolitionist and political activist. Born into slavery, she escaped in 1849 and subsequently made numerous dangerous missions to rescue enslaved Africans through the Underground Railroad. Tubman's remarkable efforts in guiding hundreds of slaves to freedom made her a leading figure in the fight against slavery. During the American Civil War, she served as a nurse, cook, and spy for the Union Army. After the war, Tubman continued her advocacy for women's suffrage and the rights of African Americans.

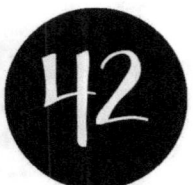

42

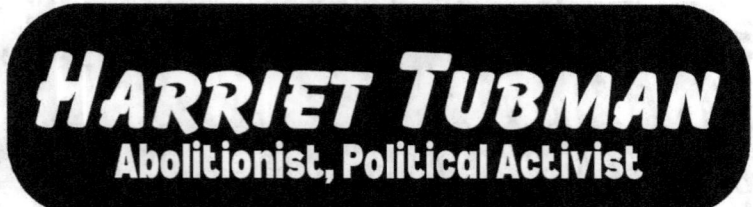

HARRIET TUBMAN
Abolitionist, Political Activist

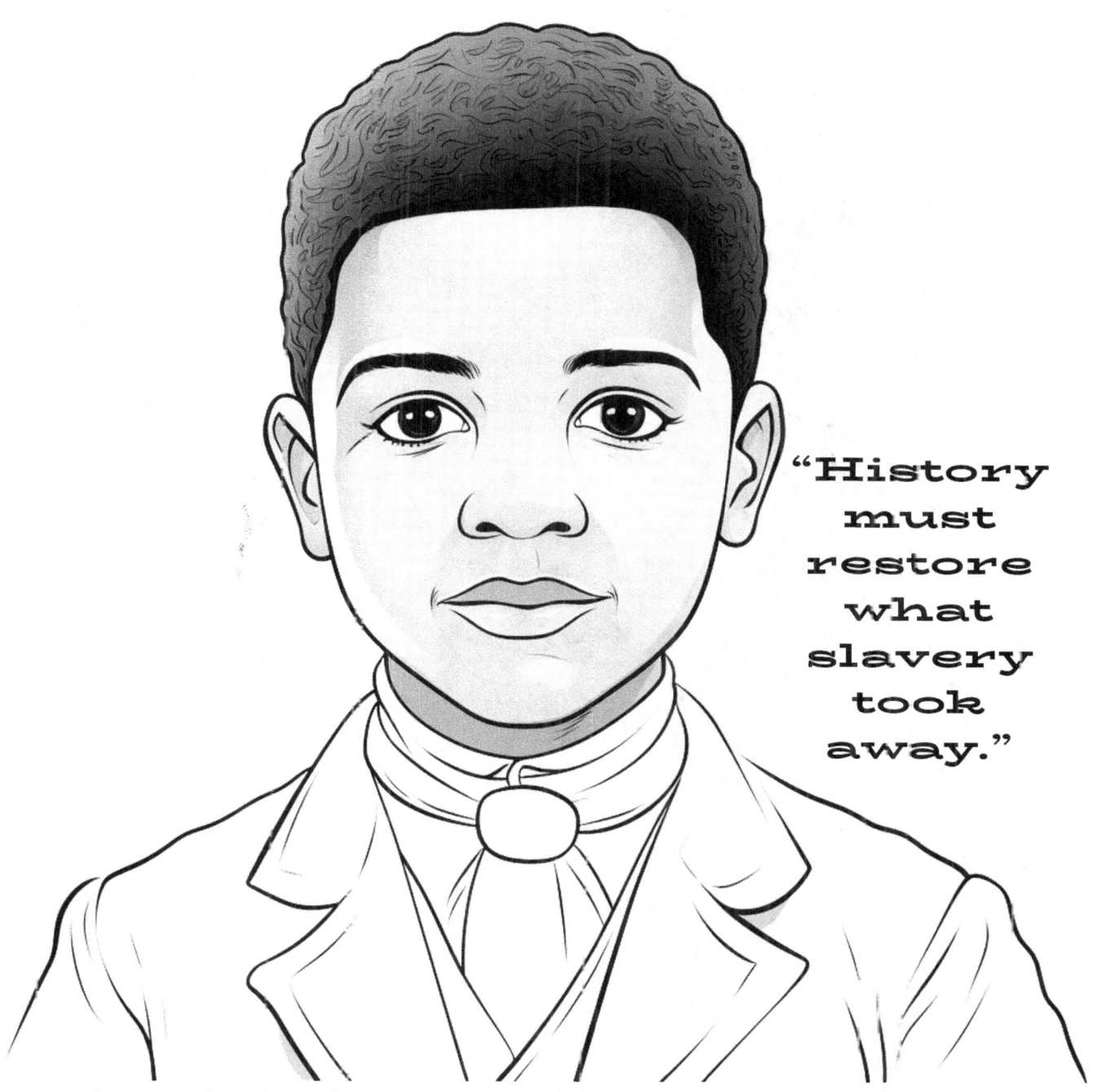

"History must restore what slavery took away."

Arturo Alfonso Schomburg (Arturo Chomburg) (January 24, 1874 – June 10, 1938) was a Puerto Rican-born writer, historian, and activist. He played a pivotal role in preserving and promoting the history and contributions of African people and people of African descent. Schomburg's personal collection of books, manuscripts, and artwork formed the foundation of the Schomburg Center for Research in Black Culture, now a branch of the New York Public Library. His tireless efforts to document and celebrate the African diaspora helped shape the field of African-American studies and inspire future generations of scholars.

ARTURO SCHOMBURG
Writer, Historian, Activist

43

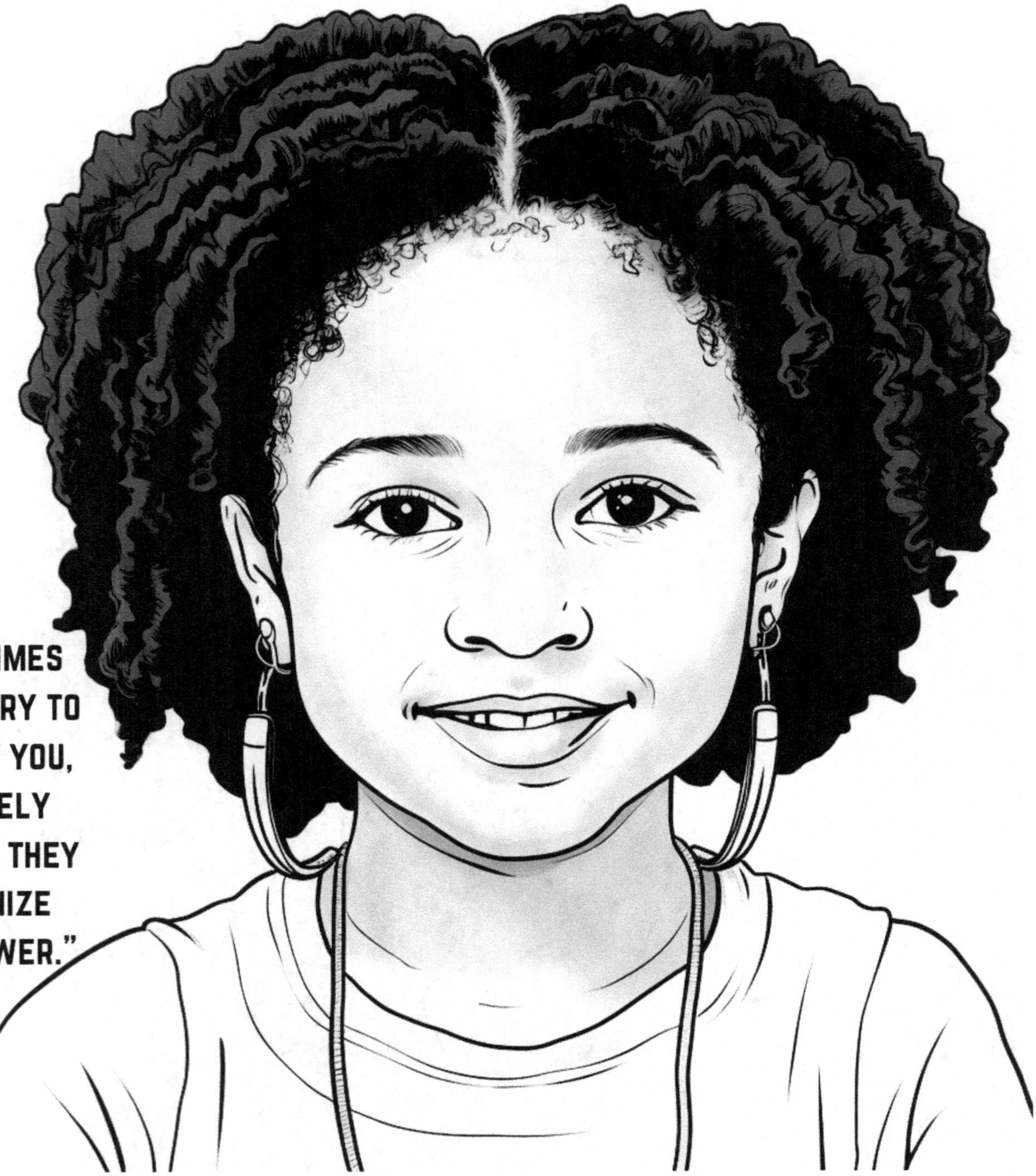

"SOMETIMES PEOPLE TRY TO DESTROY YOU, PRECISELY BECAUSE THEY RECOGNIZE YOUR POWER."

bell hooks (Gloria Jean Watkins) (September 25, 1952 – December 15, 2021) was an influential feminist scholar, cultural critic, and author. Her groundbreaking works, such as "Ain't I a Woman?: Black Women and Feminism" (1981) and "Feminist Theory: From Margin to Center" (1984), challenged traditional feminist discourse and highlighted the intersectionality of race, gender, and class. hooks' writings explore the ways in which systems of power impact marginalized communities and call for radical social and political transformation. Her work has made significant contributions to feminist theory and cultural studies.

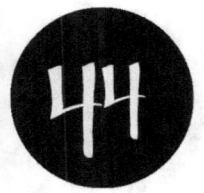

BELL HOOKS
Feminist Scholar, Cultural Critic, and Author

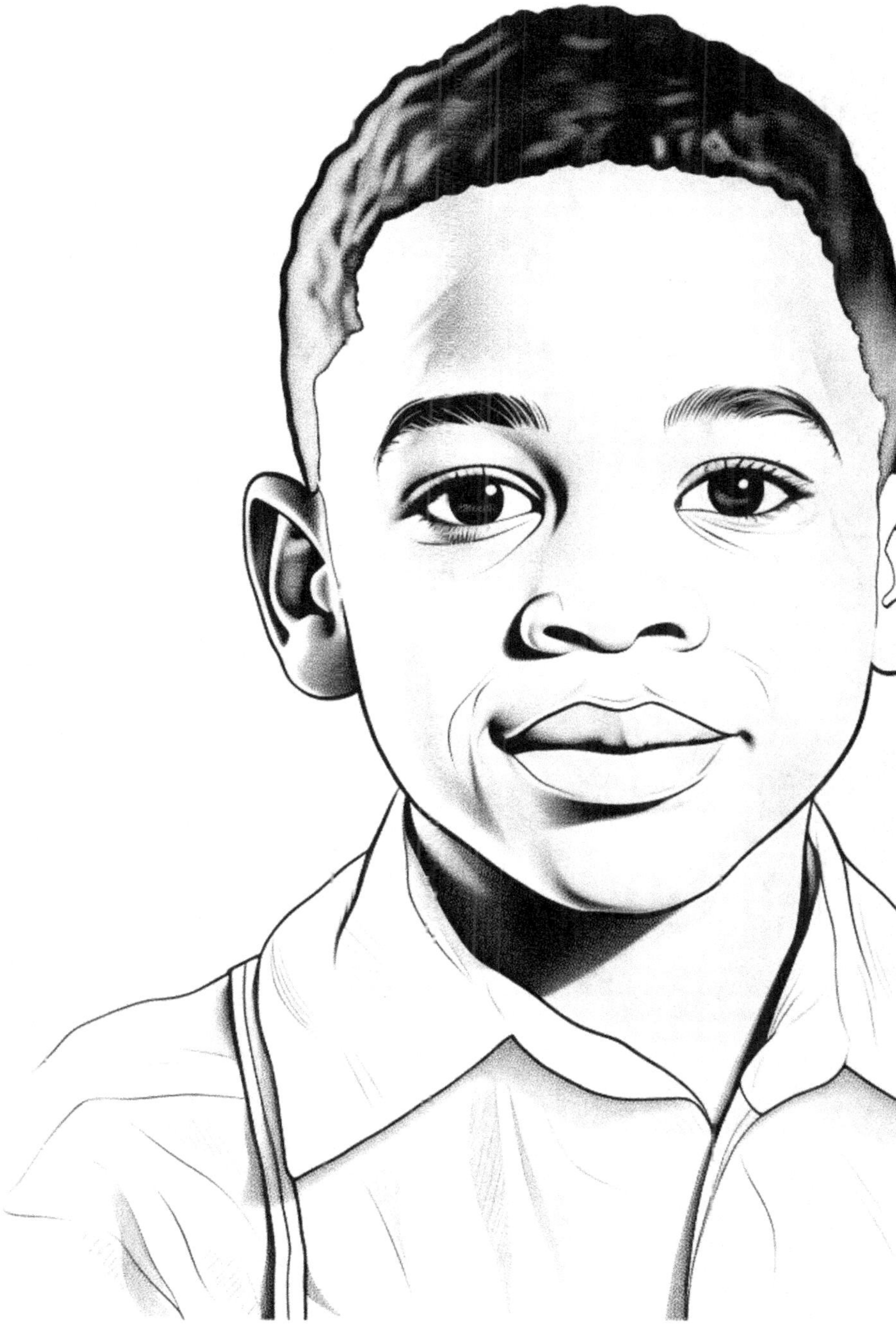

"ALL LITERATURE IS PROTEST."

Richard Wright (September 4, 1908 – November 28, 1960) was an influential writer and author. He is best known for his novel "Native Son" (1940), which brought him critical acclaim and commercial success. The novel explored themes of racial inequality and social injustice. Wright's works, including "Black Boy" (1945), a memoir of his childhood and youth in the segregated South, had a significant impact on American literature, shedding light on the experiences of African Americans and challenging prevailing racial stereotypes.

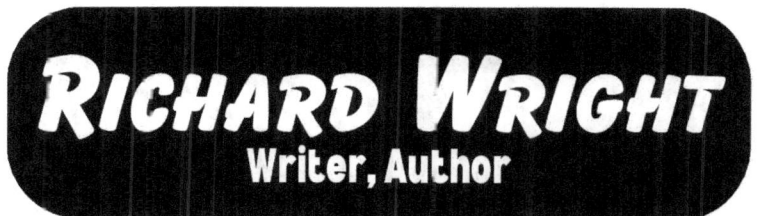

RICHARD WRIGHT
Writer, Author

45

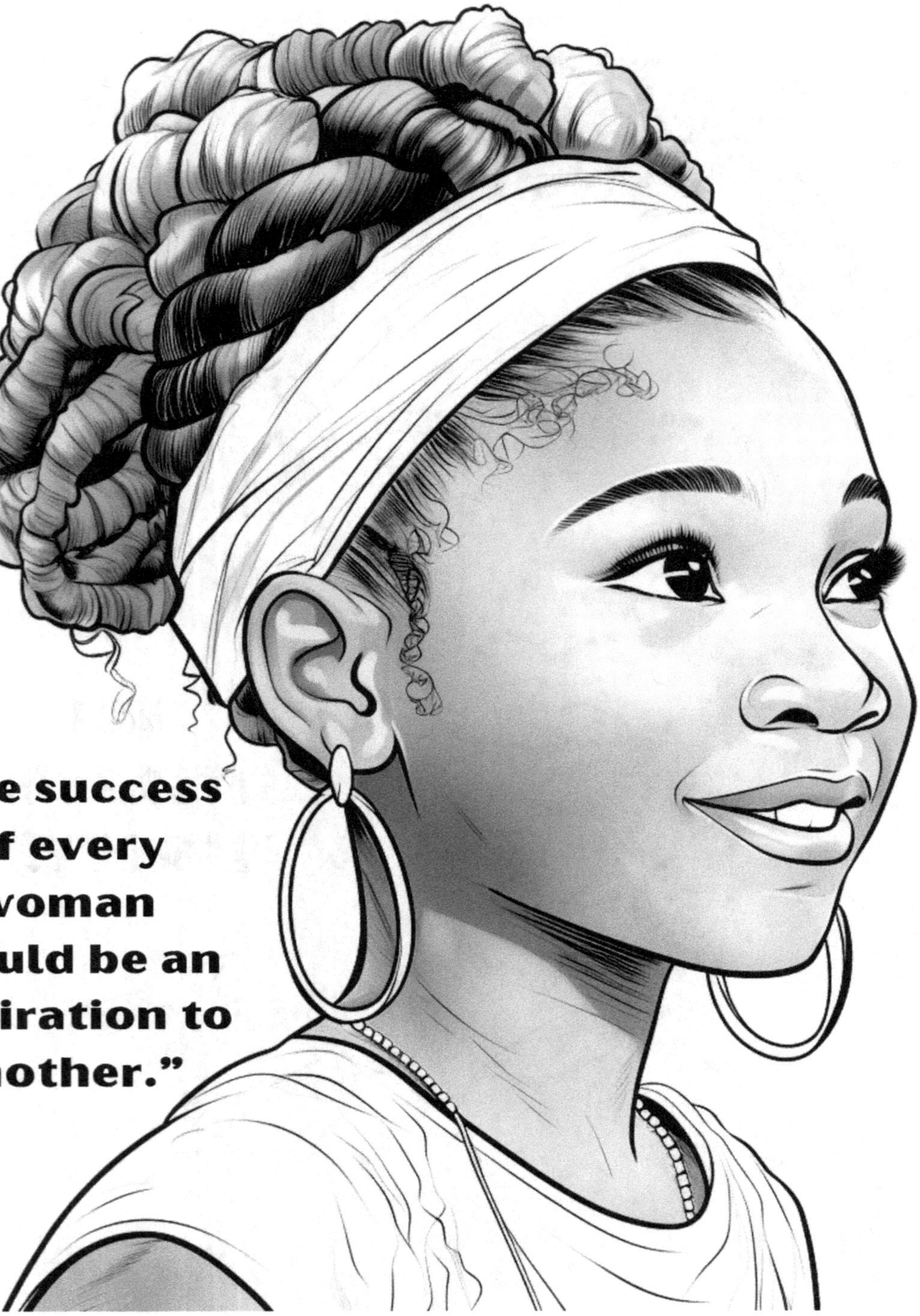

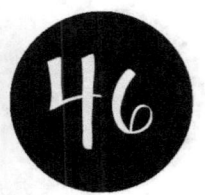

"The success of every woman should be an inspiration to another."

Serena Williams (born September 26, 1981) is a professional tennis player widely regarded as one of the greatest athletes of all time. Throughout her career, she has won numerous Grand Slam singles titles, including 23 major championships, and has held the world No. 1 ranking in women's singles on multiple occasions. Williams' exceptional athleticism, power, and dominance on the tennis court have redefined the sport. Off the court, she is known for her activism and advocacy for gender and racial equality.

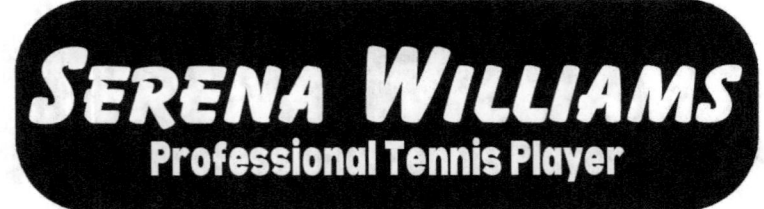

SERENA WILLIAMS
Professional Tennis Player

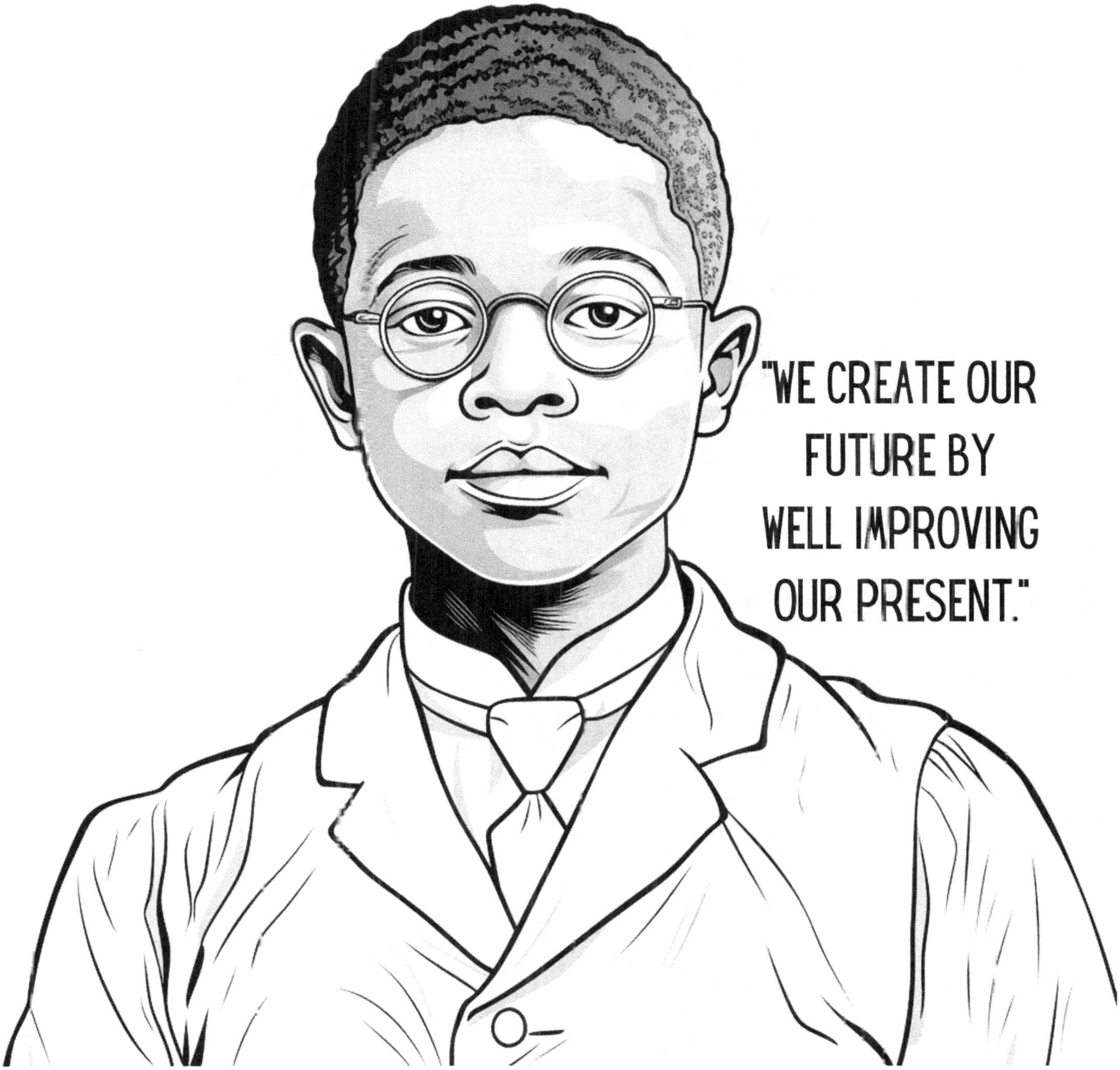

"WE CREATE OUR FUTURE BY WELL IMPROVING OUR PRESENT."

Lewis Latimer (September 4, 1848 – December 11, 1928) was an inventor and engineer who made significant contributions to the development of electric lighting. He worked closely with Thomas Edison and played a crucial role in the patenting and improvement of the incandescent light bulb. Latimer also invented an improved carbon filament that made light bulbs more durable and efficient. His expertise in electrical engineering and drafting skills were highly regarded, and he worked on various other inventions throughout his career.

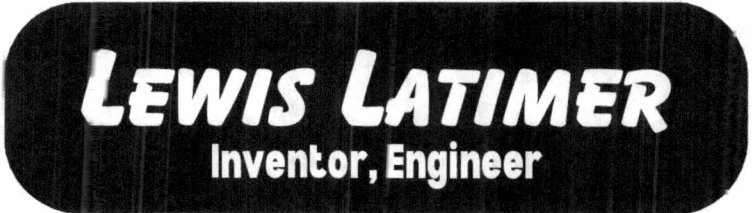

LEWIS LATIMER
Inventor, Engineer

47

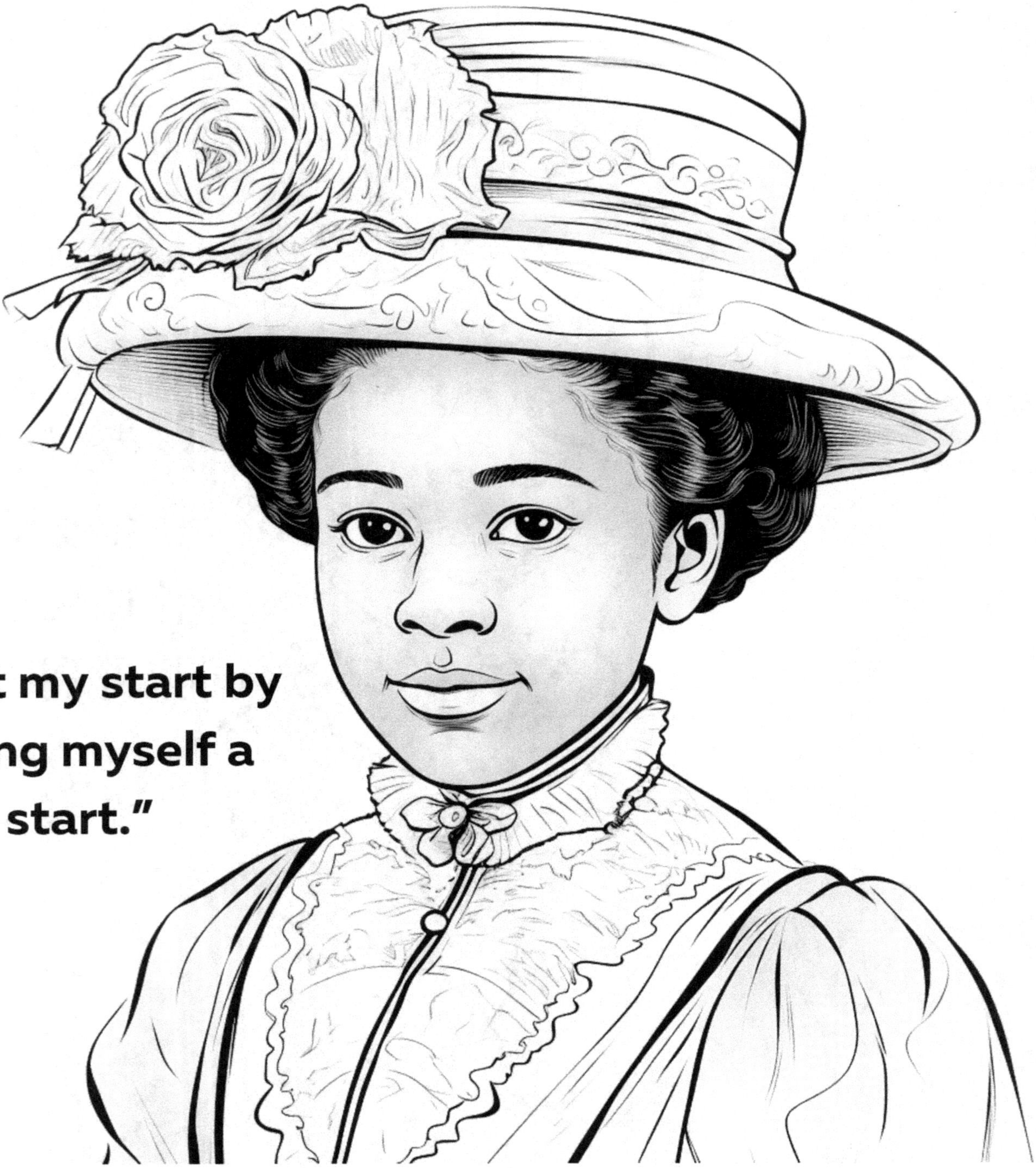

"I got my start by giving myself a start."

Madam C.J. Walker (Sarah Breedlove Walker) (December 23, 1867 – May 25, 1919) was an entrepreneur, philanthropist, and the first female self-made millionaire in the United States. Born into poverty, Walker developed and marketed a line of hair care products specifically designed for African-American women. Through her innovative business practices and savvy marketing strategies, she built a successful cosmetics empire. Walker's accomplishments as a businesswoman and her philanthropic efforts to support education and social causes made her an influential figure in both business and the African-American community.

48

MADAM C.J. WALKER
Entrepreneur, Philanthropist, Self-Made Millionaire

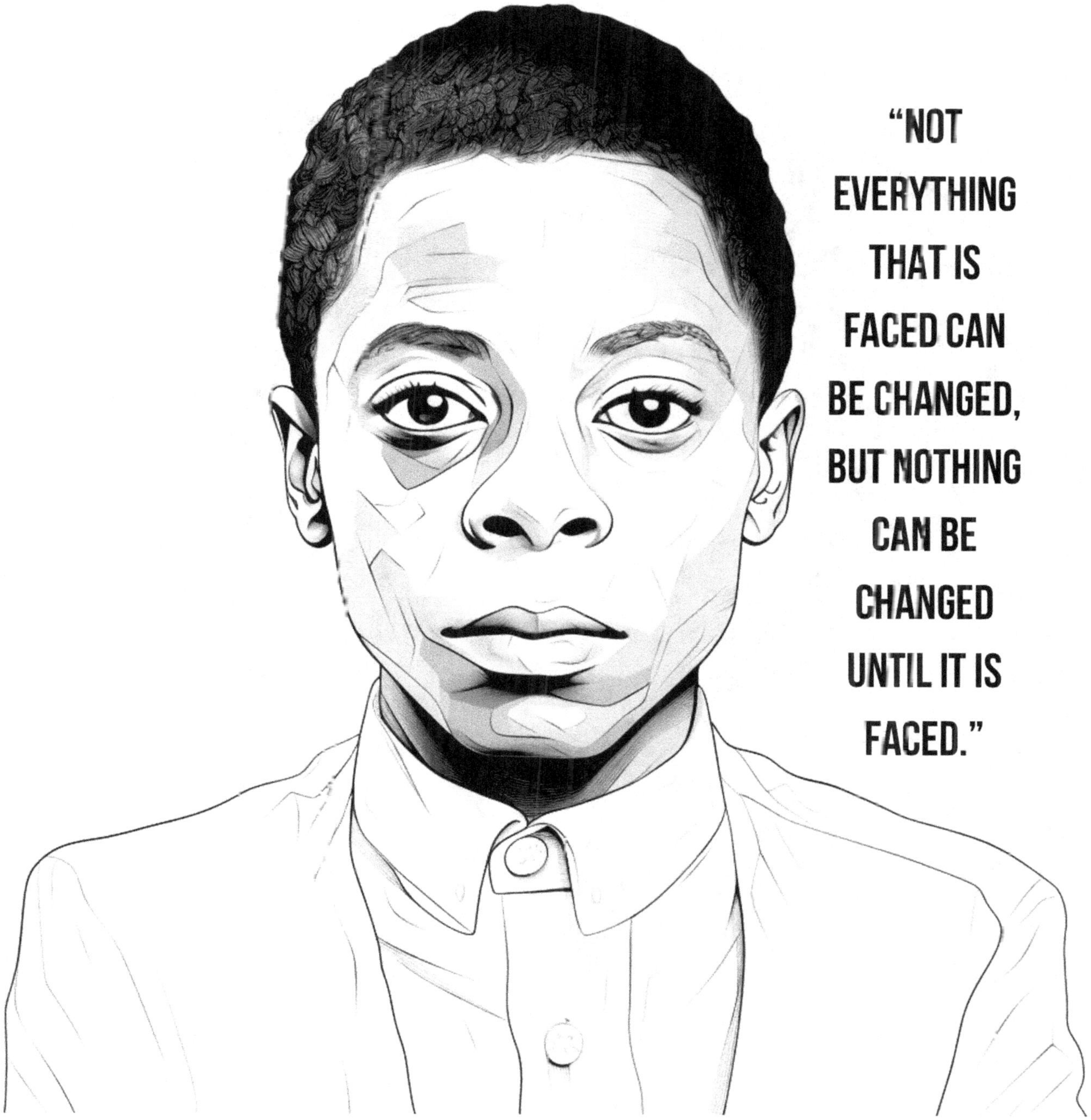

"NOT EVERYTHING THAT IS FACED CAN BE CHANGED, BUT NOTHING CAN BE CHANGED UNTIL IT IS FACED."

James Arthur Baldwin (August 2, 1924 – December 1, 1987) was a novelist, essayist, playwright, and social critic. Born in Harlem, New York City, Baldwin's childhood experiences with racism and poverty profoundly influenced his writing. He became an influential voice in the civil rights movement and used his literary talent to address issues of race, sexuality, and identity. In addition to his contributions to the civil rights movement, Baldwin was an early and outspoken advocate for LGBTQ+ rights, openly discussing his own homosexuality in his writings.

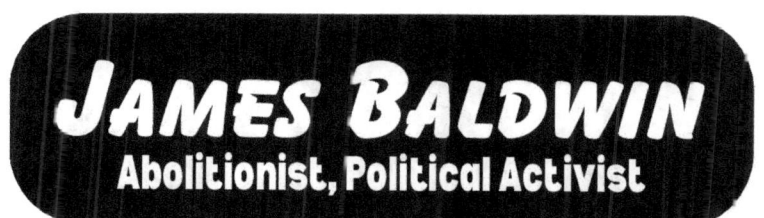

JAMES BALDWIN
Abolitionist, Political Activist

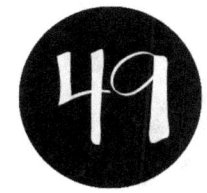

49

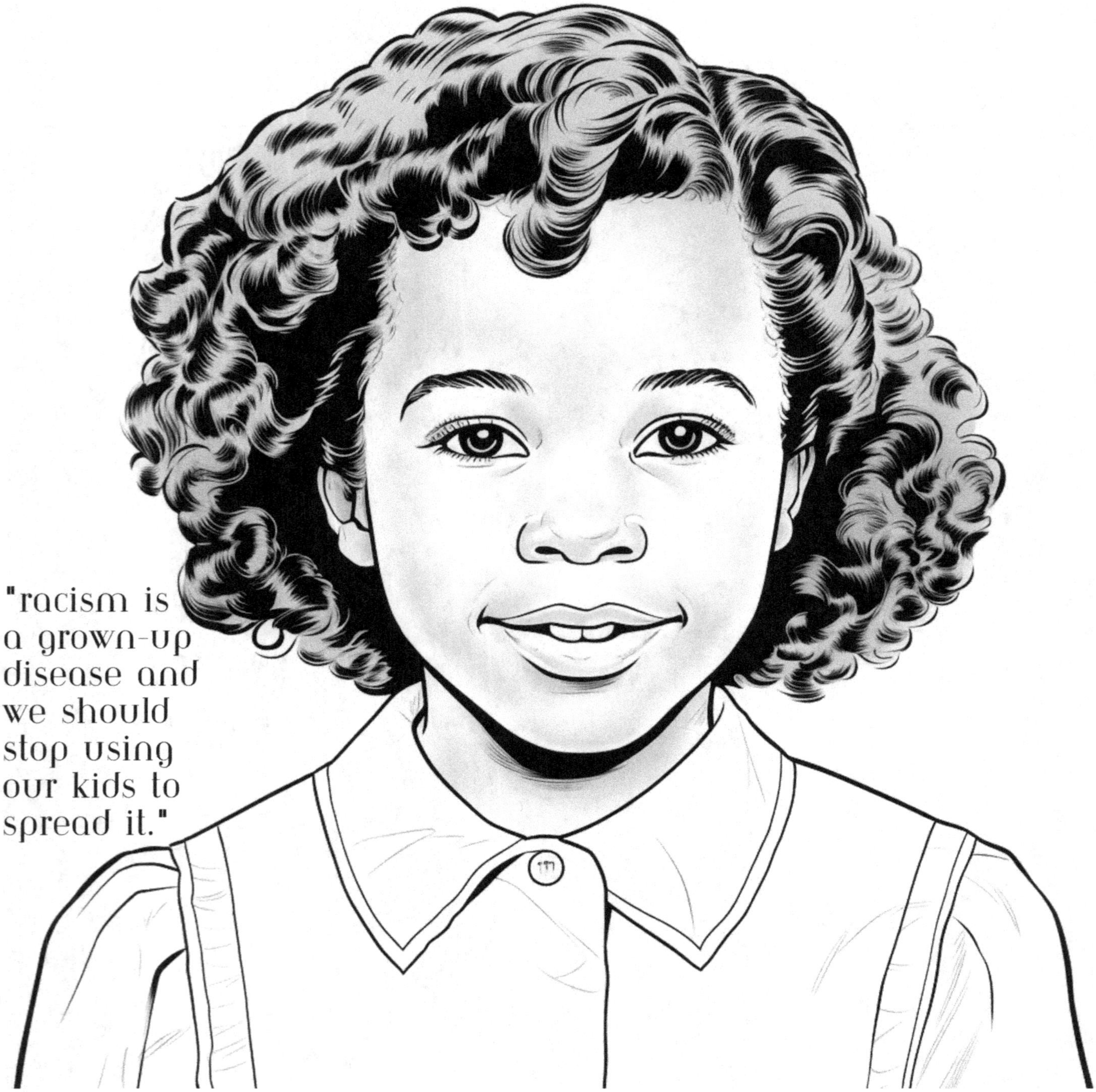

"racism is a grown-up disease and we should stop using our kids to spread it."

Ruby Bridges (born September 8, 1954) is a civil rights activist who, at the age of six, became the first African-American student to integrate an all-white elementary school in New Orleans in 1960. Despite facing violent protests and harassment, Bridges showed remarkable courage and resilience. Her bravery paved the way for the desegregation of schools across the United States and served as a symbol of the struggle for equal education. Bridges continues to advocate for equality and educational opportunities for all children.

RUBY BRIDGES
Civil Rights Activist

DOLPHINS AT PLAY

IN THE OCEAN

COLORING BOOK

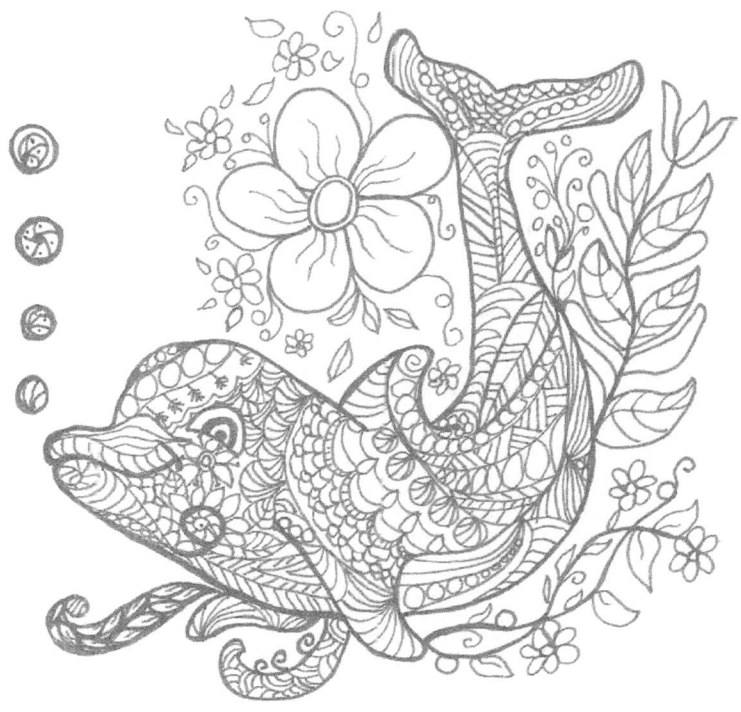

By: Kaye Dennan

KD Coloring Studio

http://kdcoloring.com

ISBN-13: 9781530536214

KD COLORING STUDIO

PUBLISHERS NOTES
Disclaimer

Paperback Edition

Manufactured in the United States of America

A note from the Author/Illustrator

The images you have to color are just a guide, feel free to add or detract from the picture as you so wish. Creating your very own style can be fun and very satisfying.

Every second page has been left blank so that you do not ruin one of your colored designs with color bleeding through the back of the page.

If you are using pencils then I would suggest you slide a piece of thin cardboard or thick paper under the page you are coloring just to prevent any pressure marks on the following page.

ABOUT DOLPHINS

Dolphins are a very popular mammal and even more so today because we can now travel to places where you can swim with dolphins and this has increased their popularity no end.

Dolphins range in size from the 1.7 metres (5.6 ft) long and 50 kilograms (110 lb) of Maui's dolphin to the 9.5 metres (31 ft) and 10 metric tons (11 short tons) killer whale. In several species the males are larger than females.

They have streamlined bodies and two limbs that are modified into flippers. Some dolphins can travel at 55.5 kilometres per hour (34.5 mph) and travel long distances.

Dolphins use their conical shaped teeth to capture fast moving prey and largely feed on squid and fish. They have well-developed hearing – their hearing is adapted for both air and water. Some species are well adapted for diving to great depths and have a layer of fat, or blubber, under the skin to keep warm in the cold water.

Most species of dolphin prefer the warmer waters of the tropical zones and it is quite common to see them near beaches and swimming alongside yachts and other boats. They will often accompany boats for quite long distances, swimming near the bow of the boat and up in front of it.

Male dolphins typically mate with multiple females every year, but females only mate every two to three years. Calves are typically born in the spring and summer months and females bear all the responsibility for raising them. Mothers often nurse their young for a relatively long period of time.

Dolphins produce a variety of vocalizations, usually in the form of clicks and whistles. These calling sounds can actually be quite loud and easy to hear if they are travelling alongside you when boating.

We tend to be very familiar with the bottlenose dolphin because that is the species that is most often kept in captivity and trained to perform tricks.

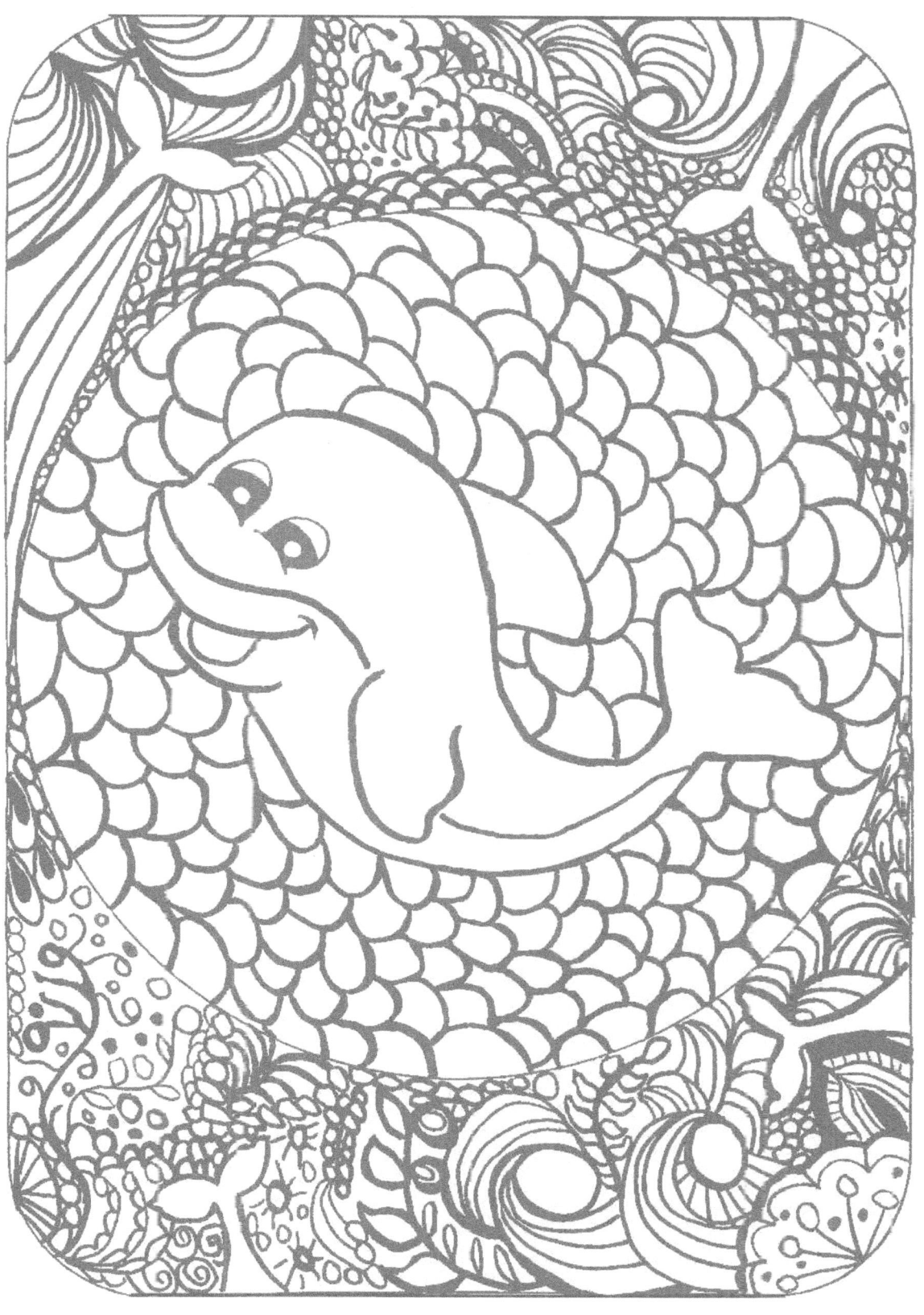

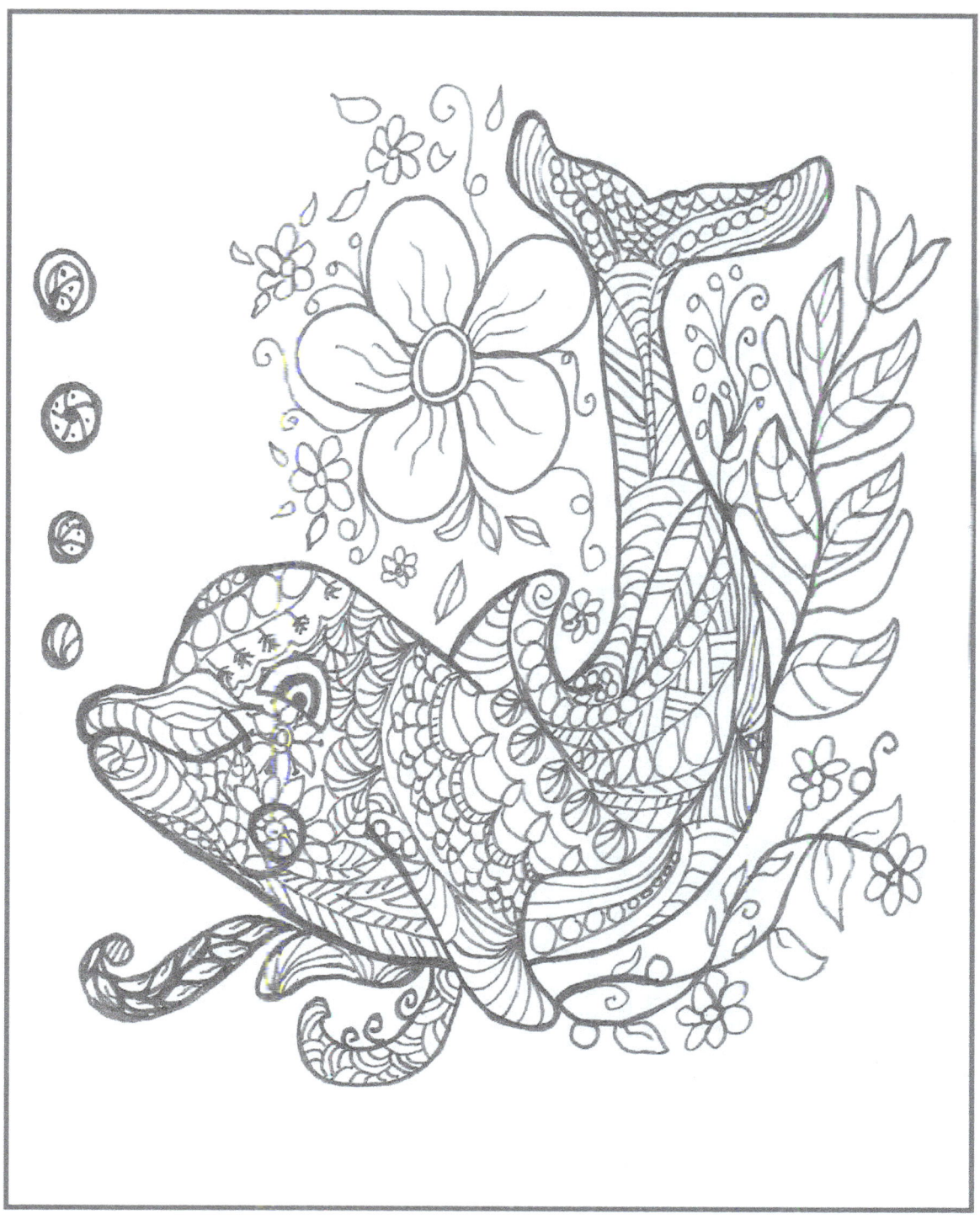

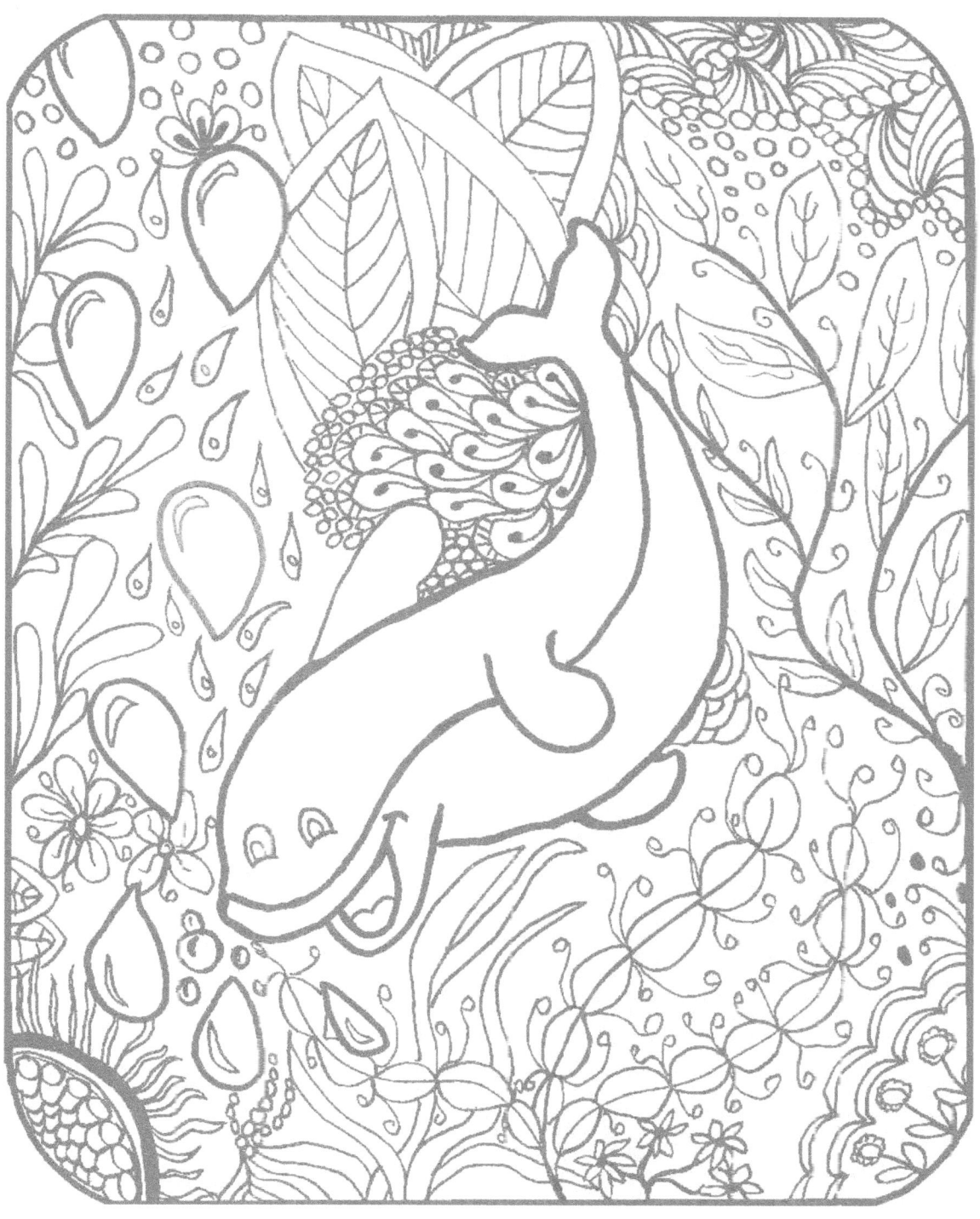

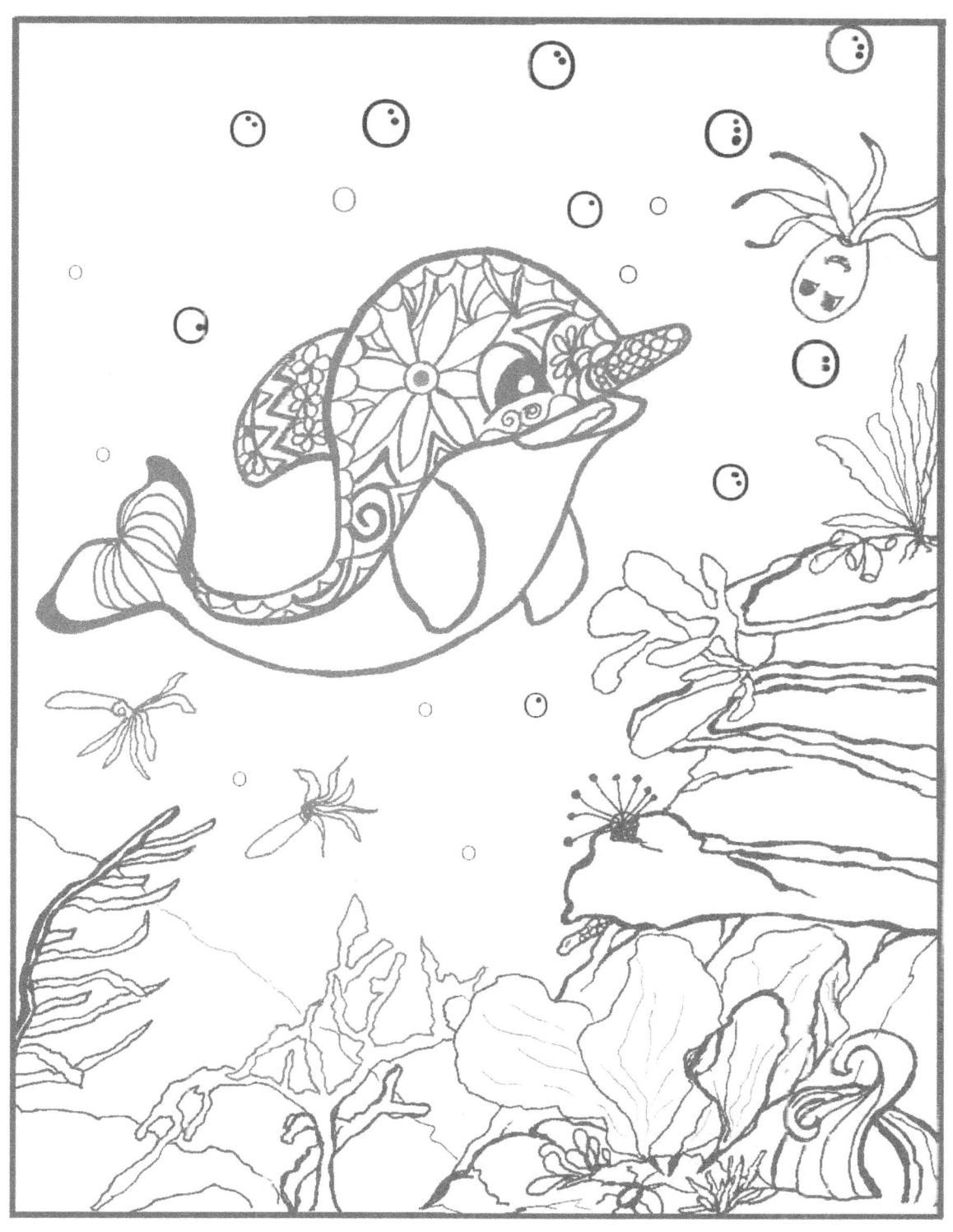

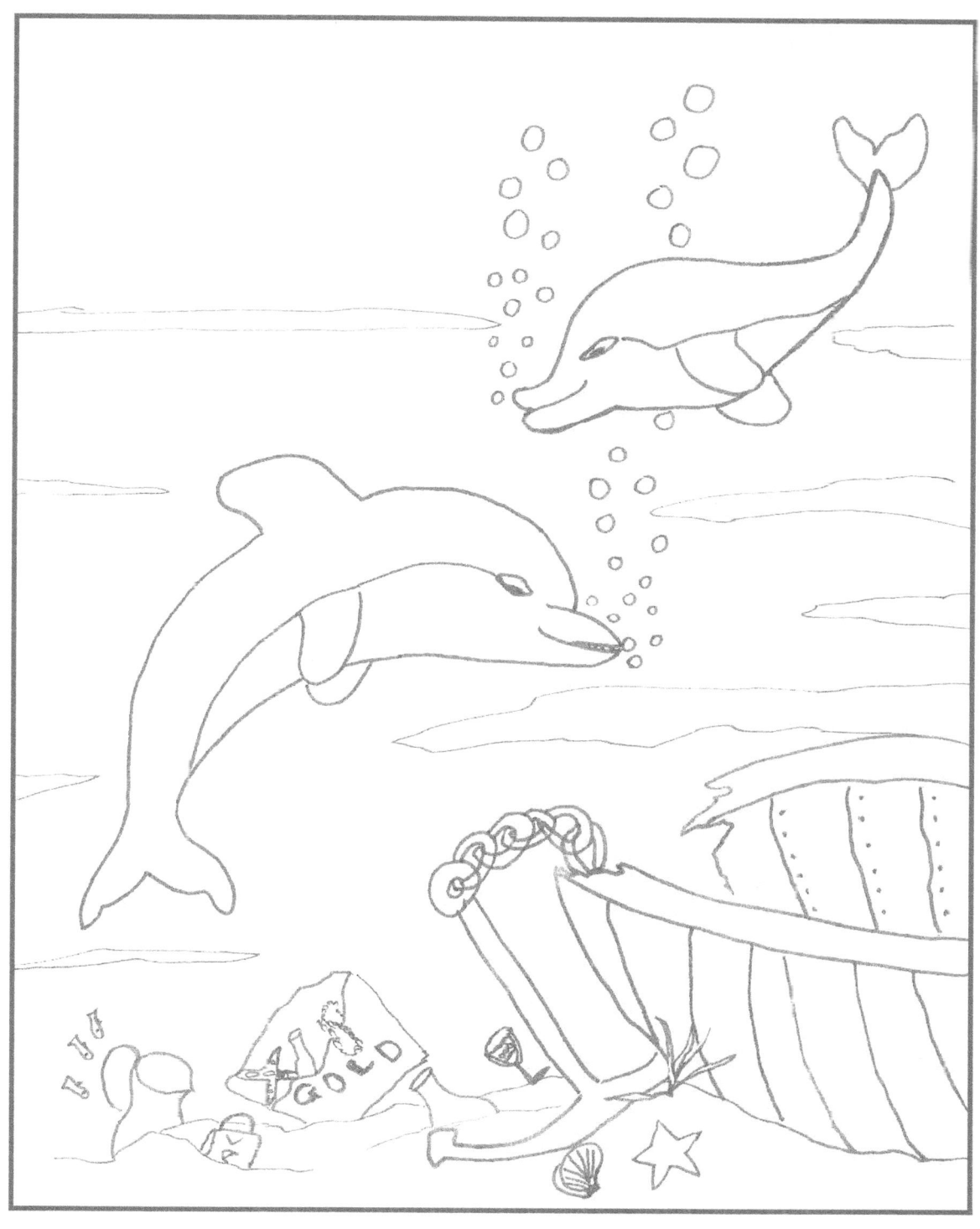

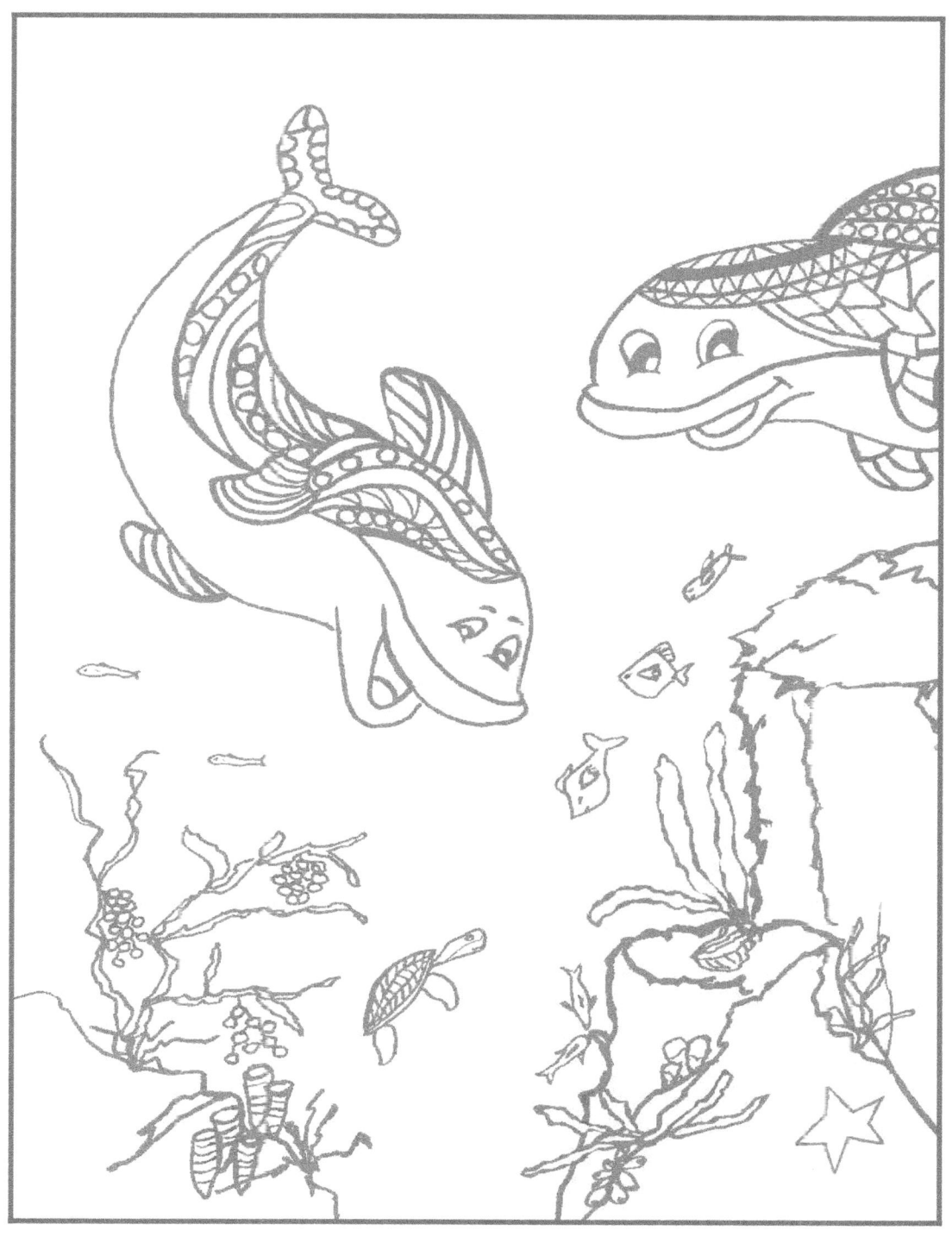

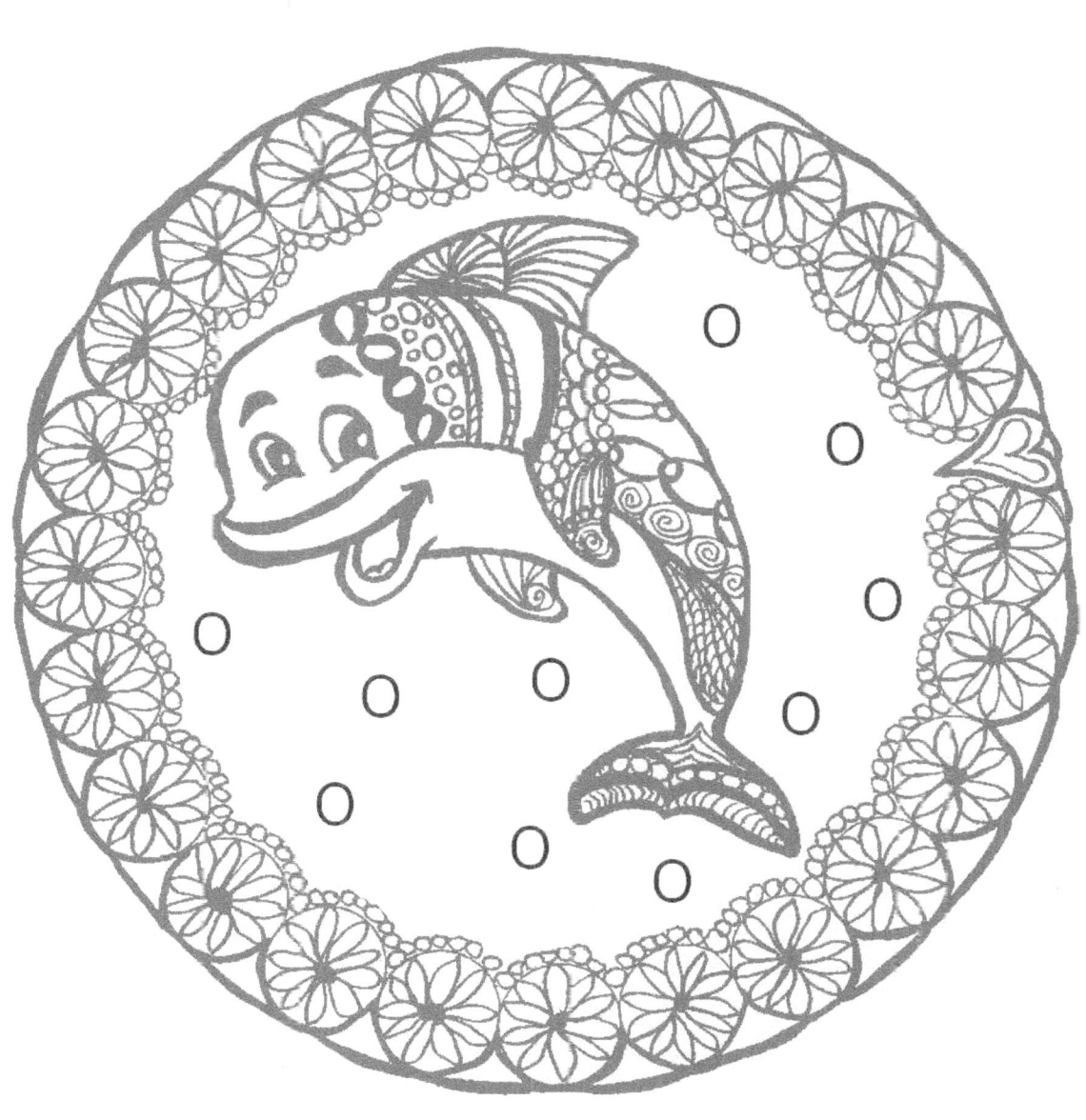

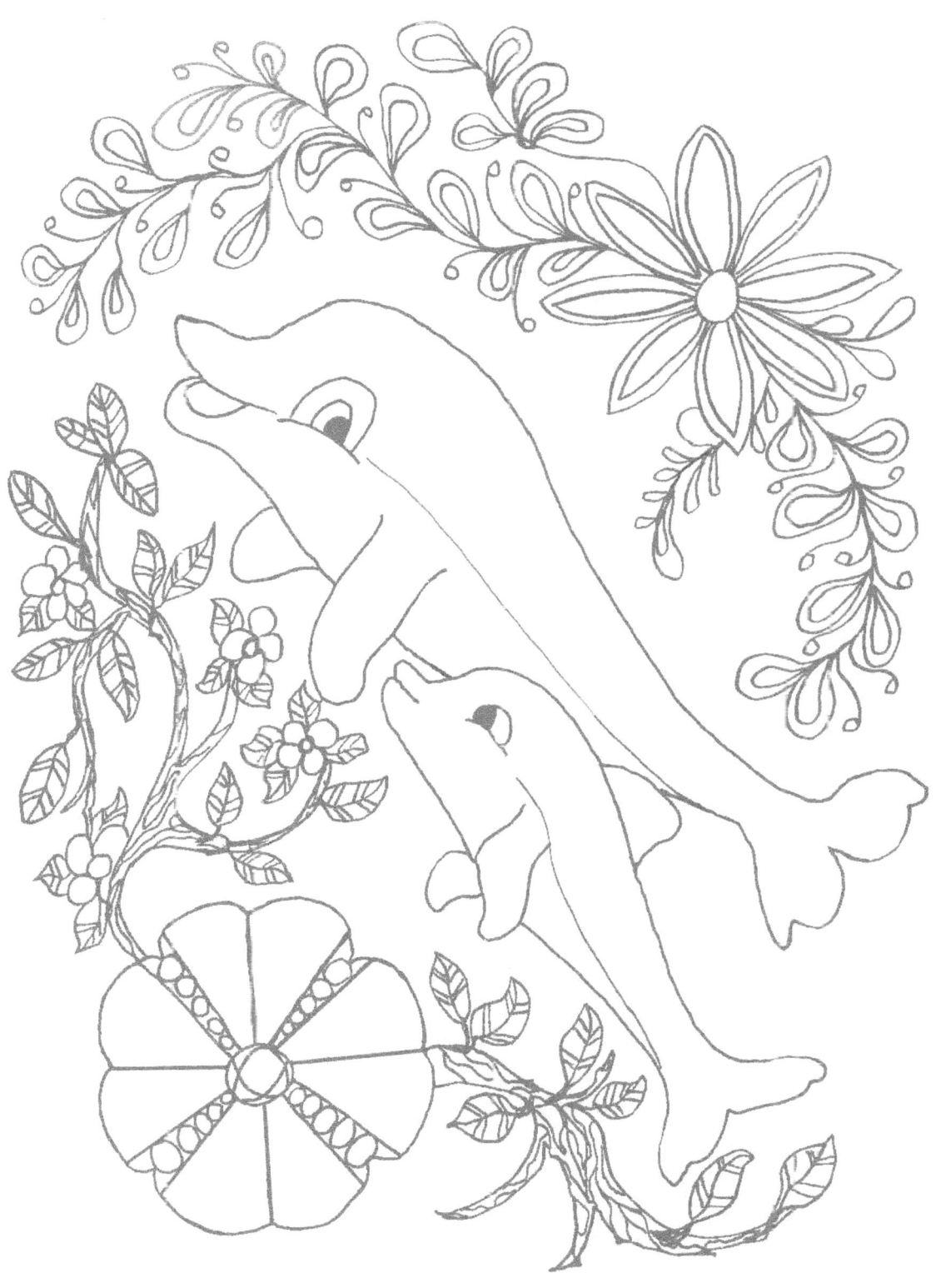

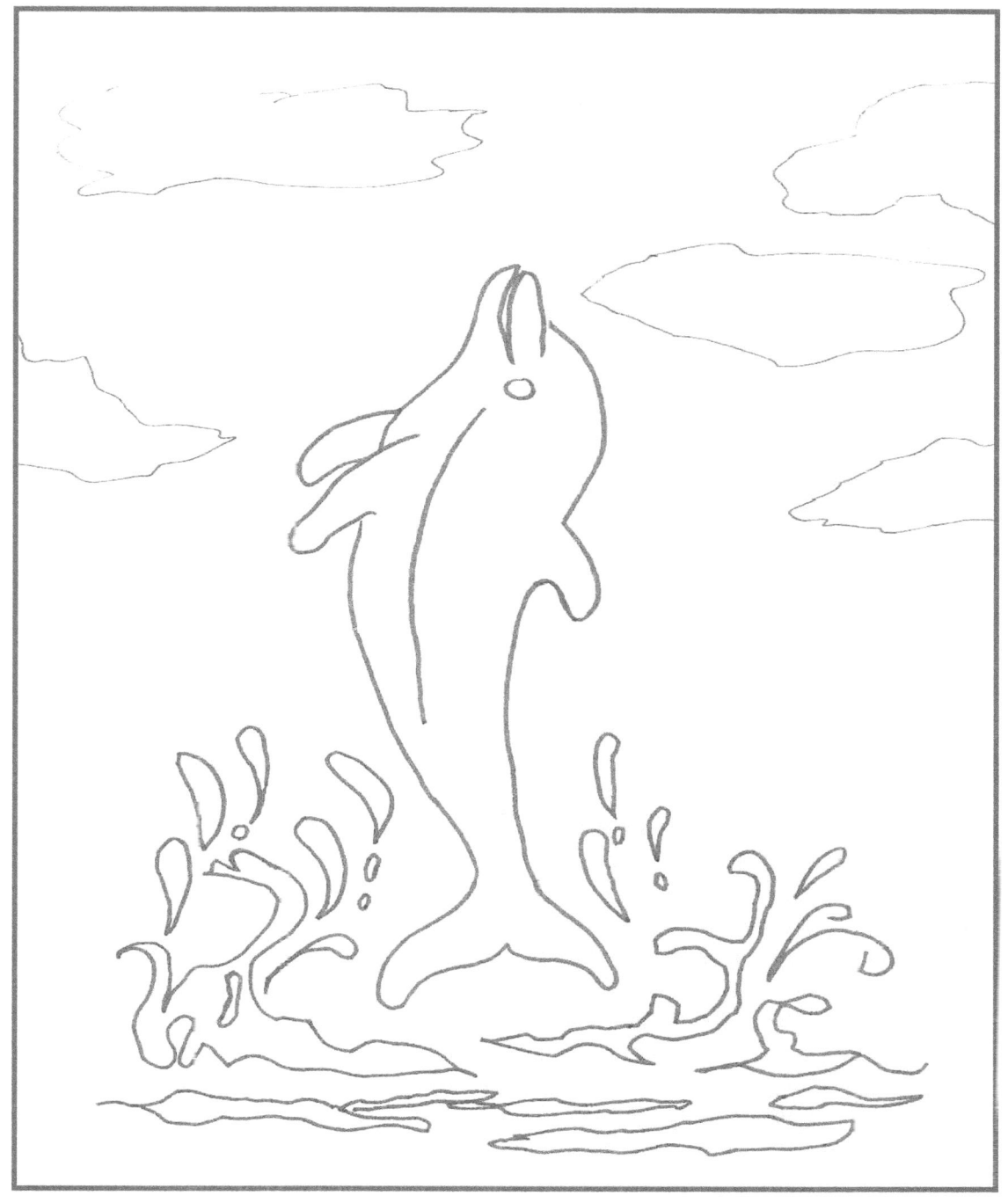

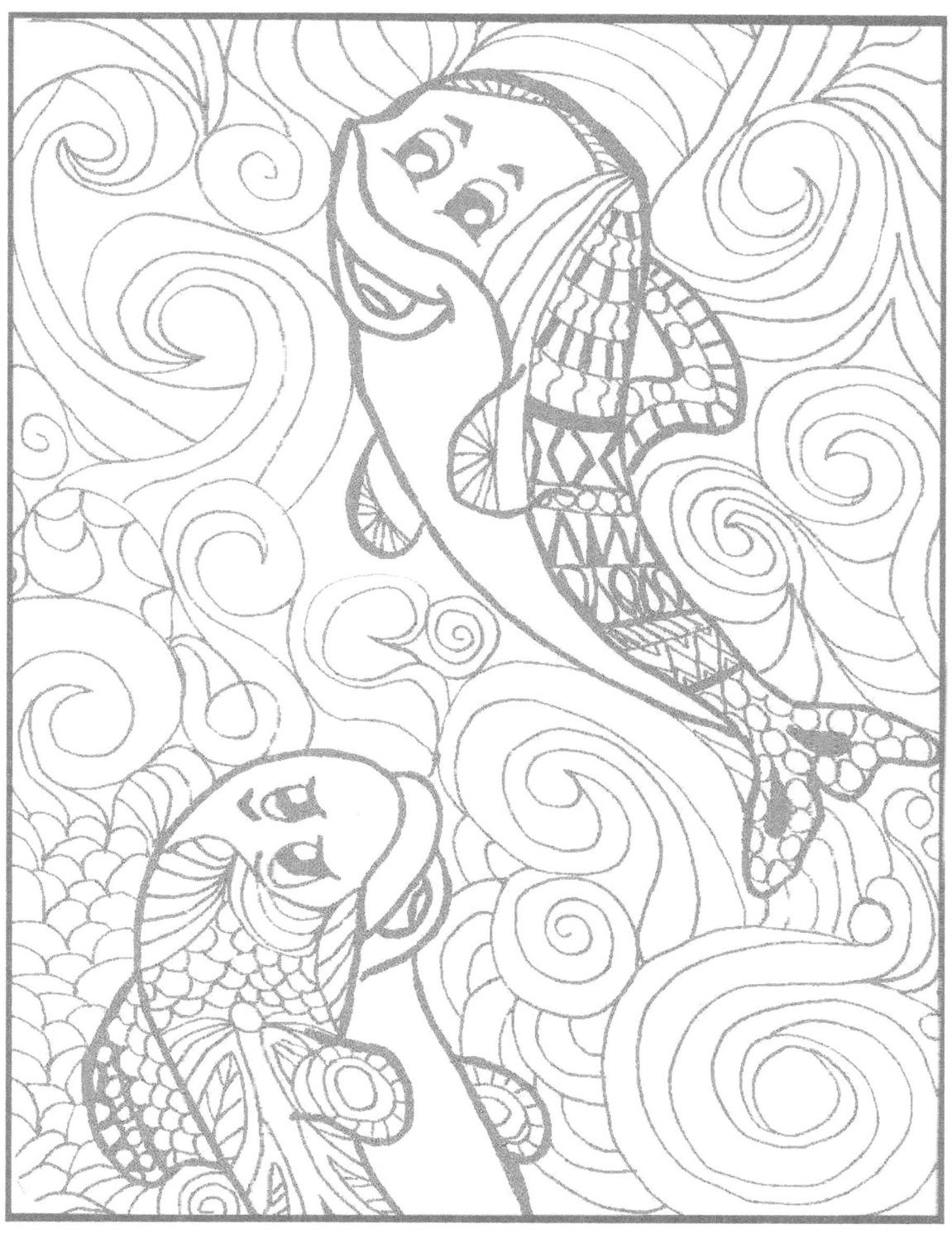

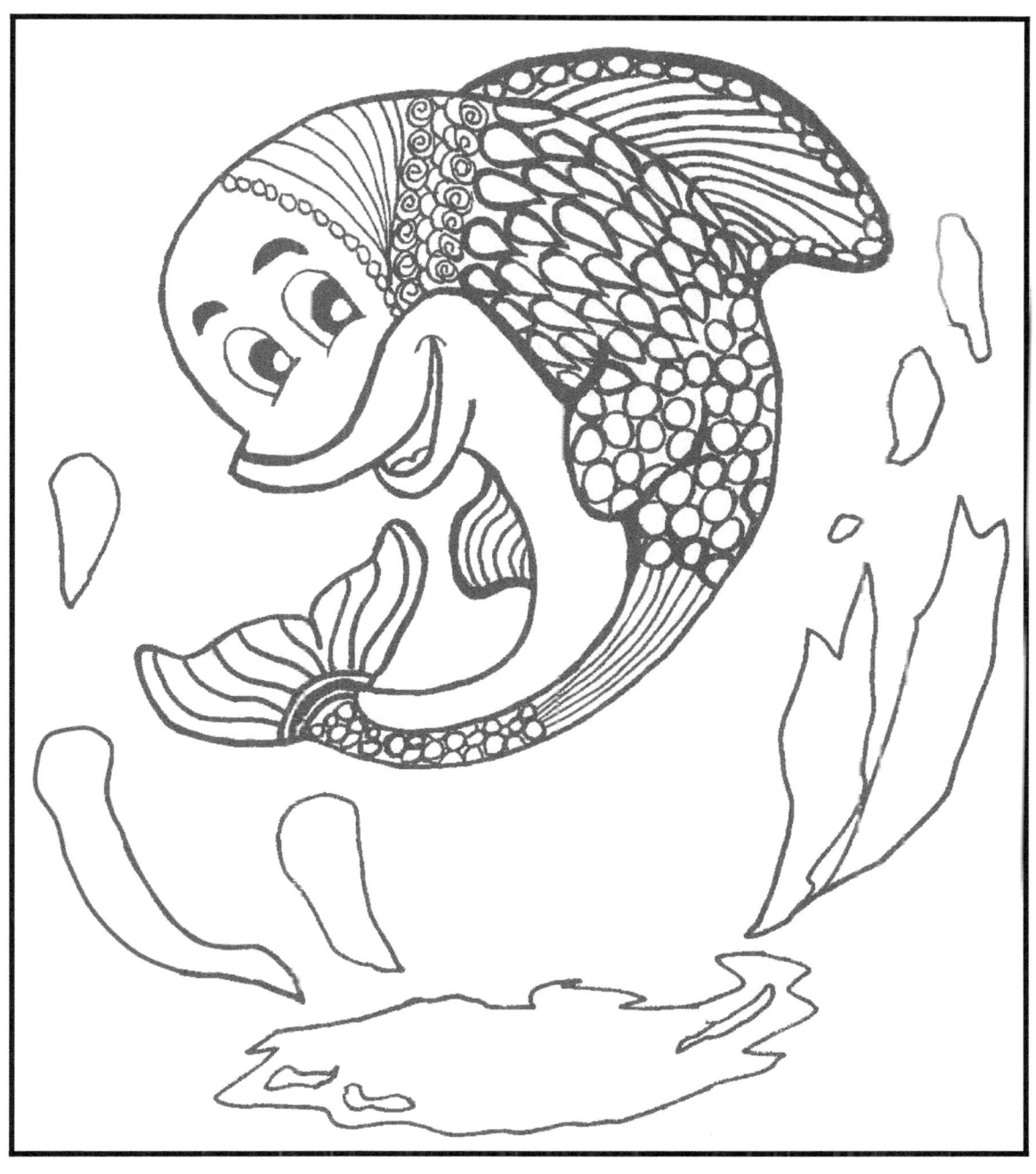

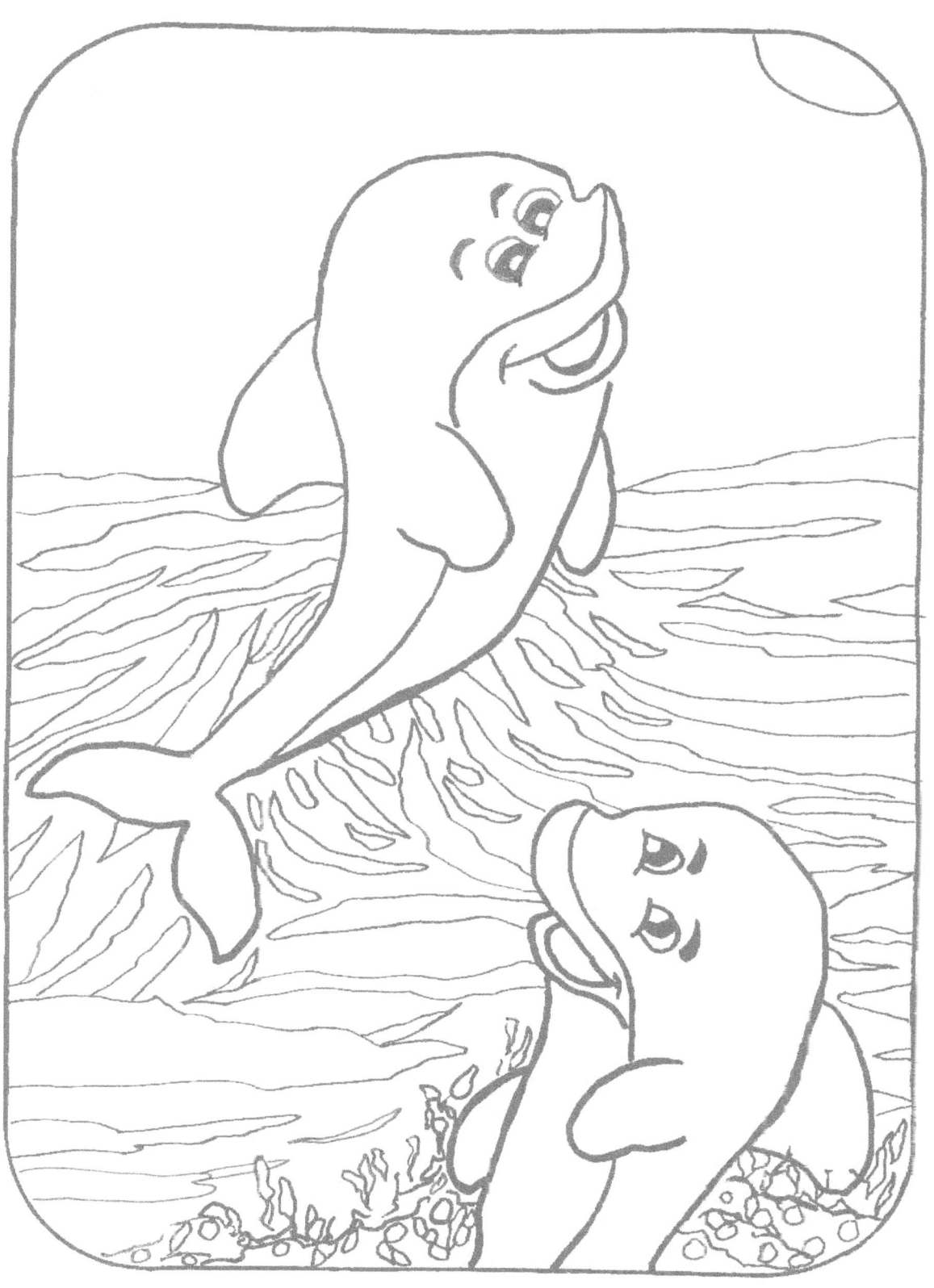

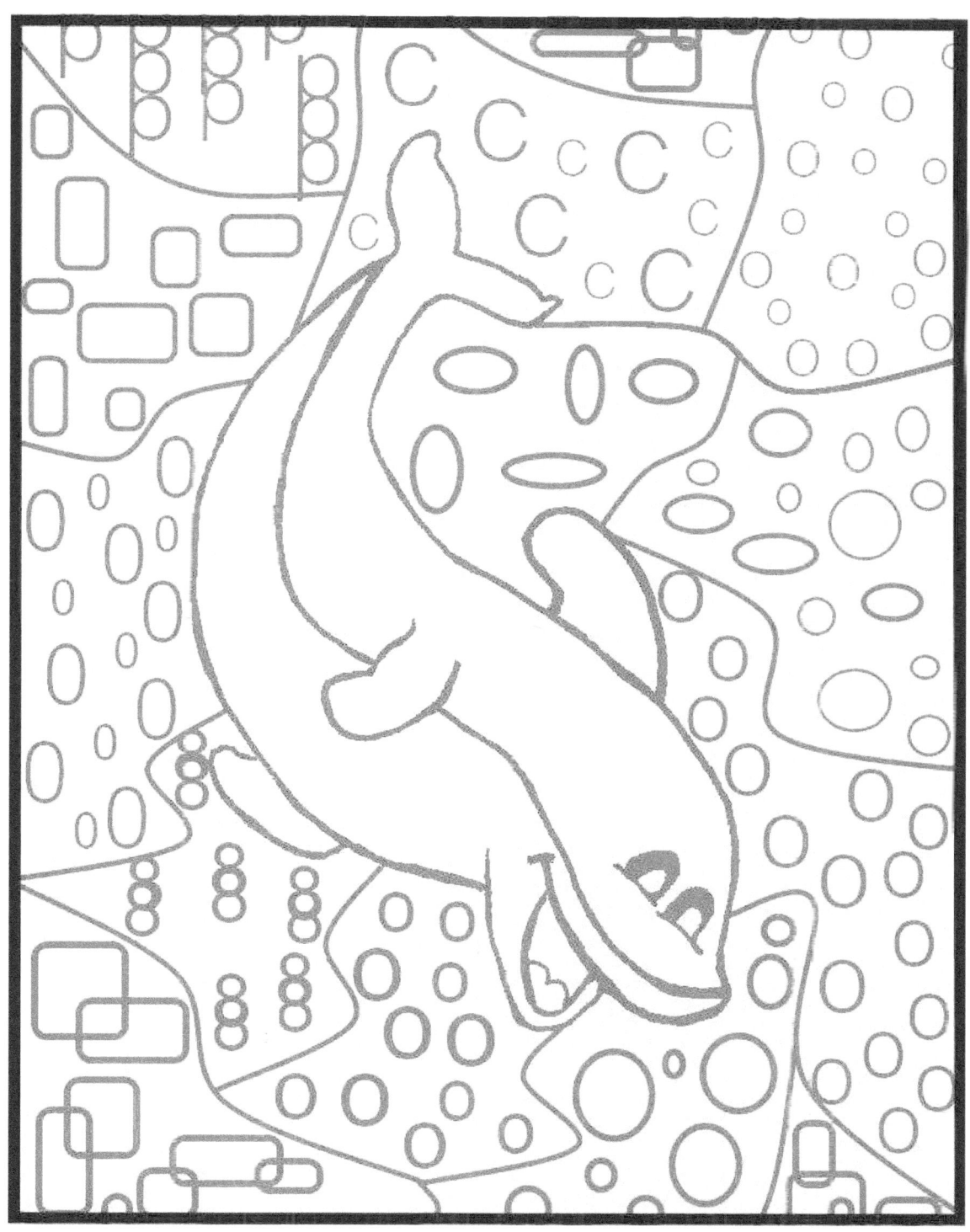

Kaye Dennan

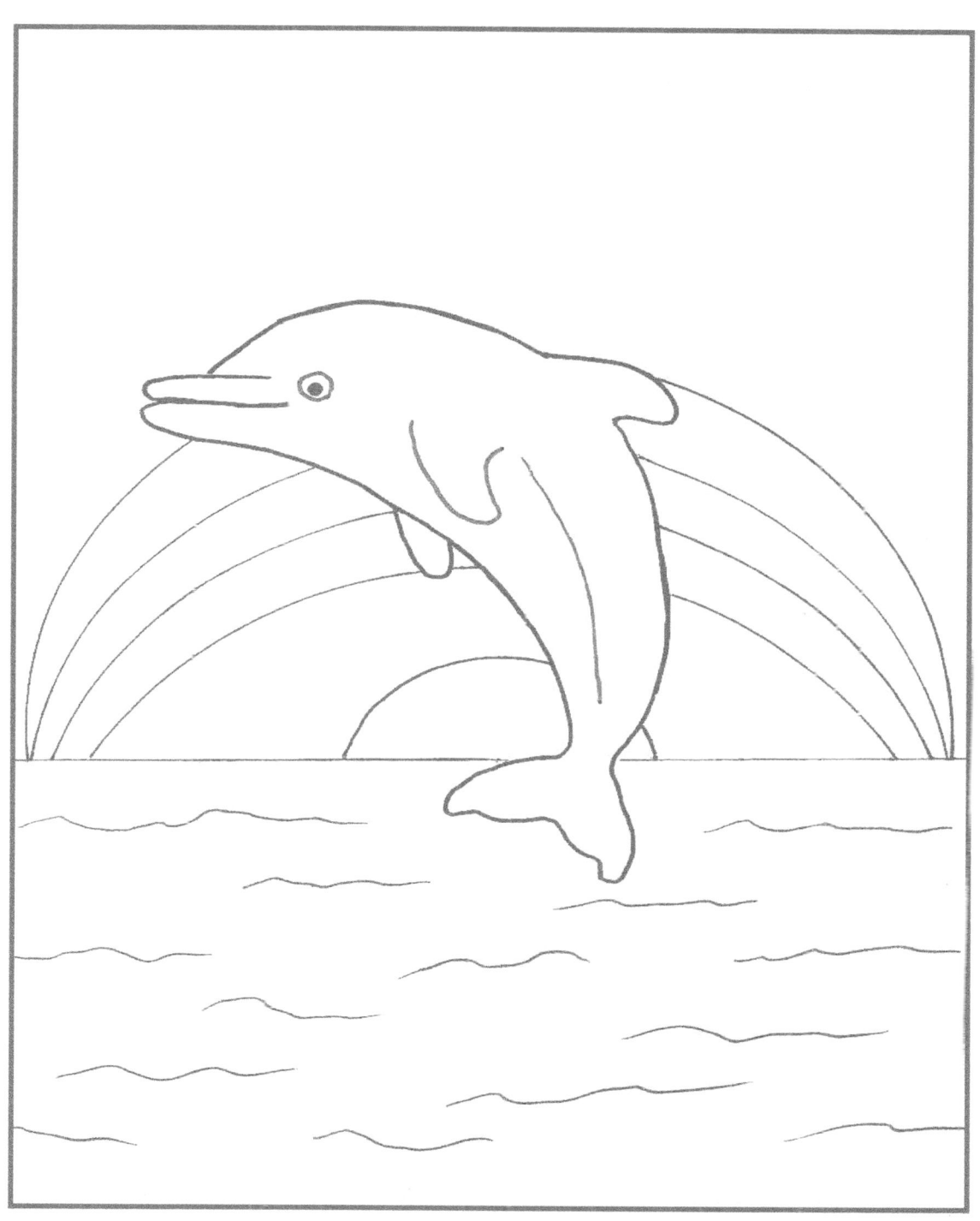

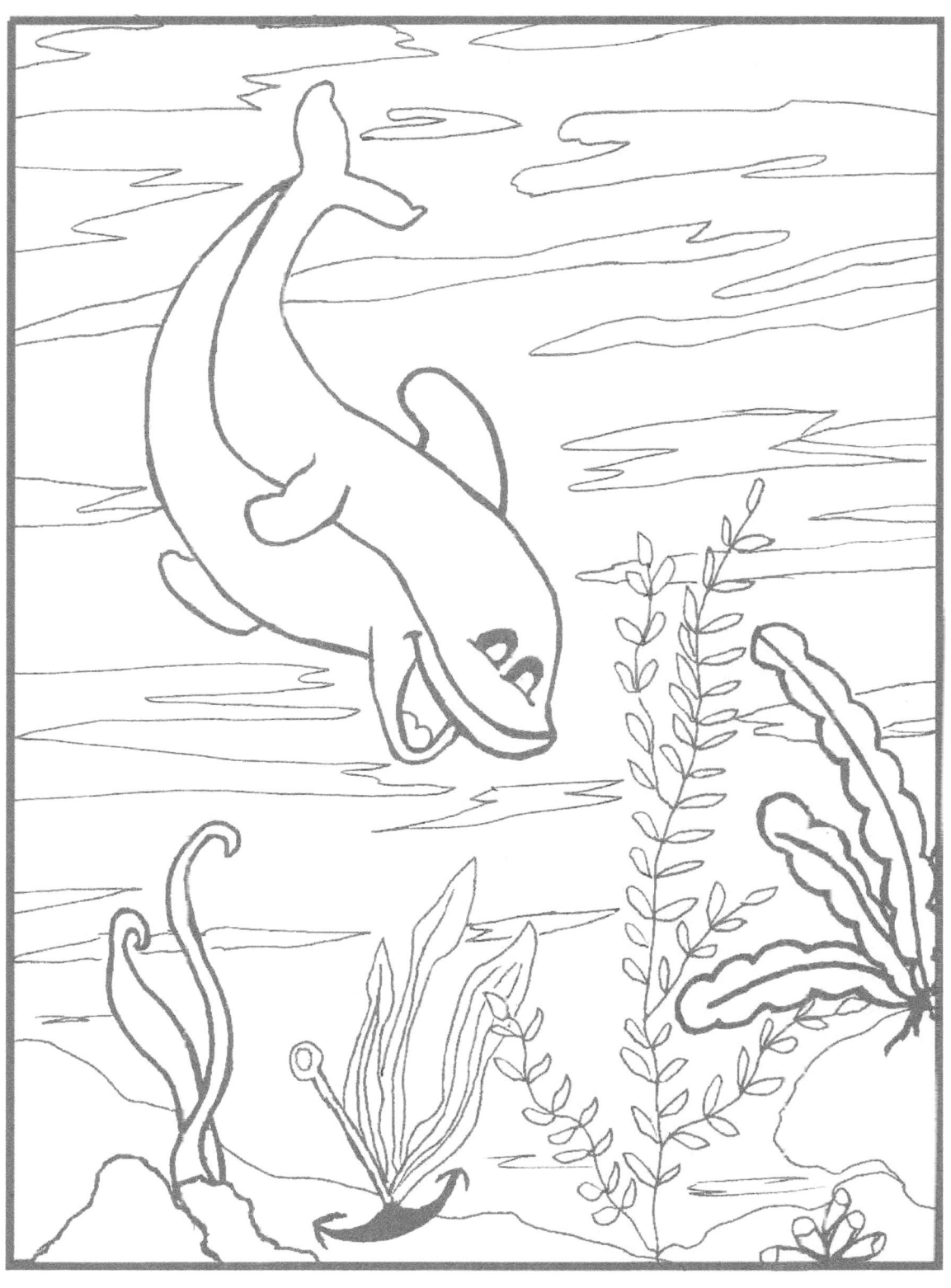

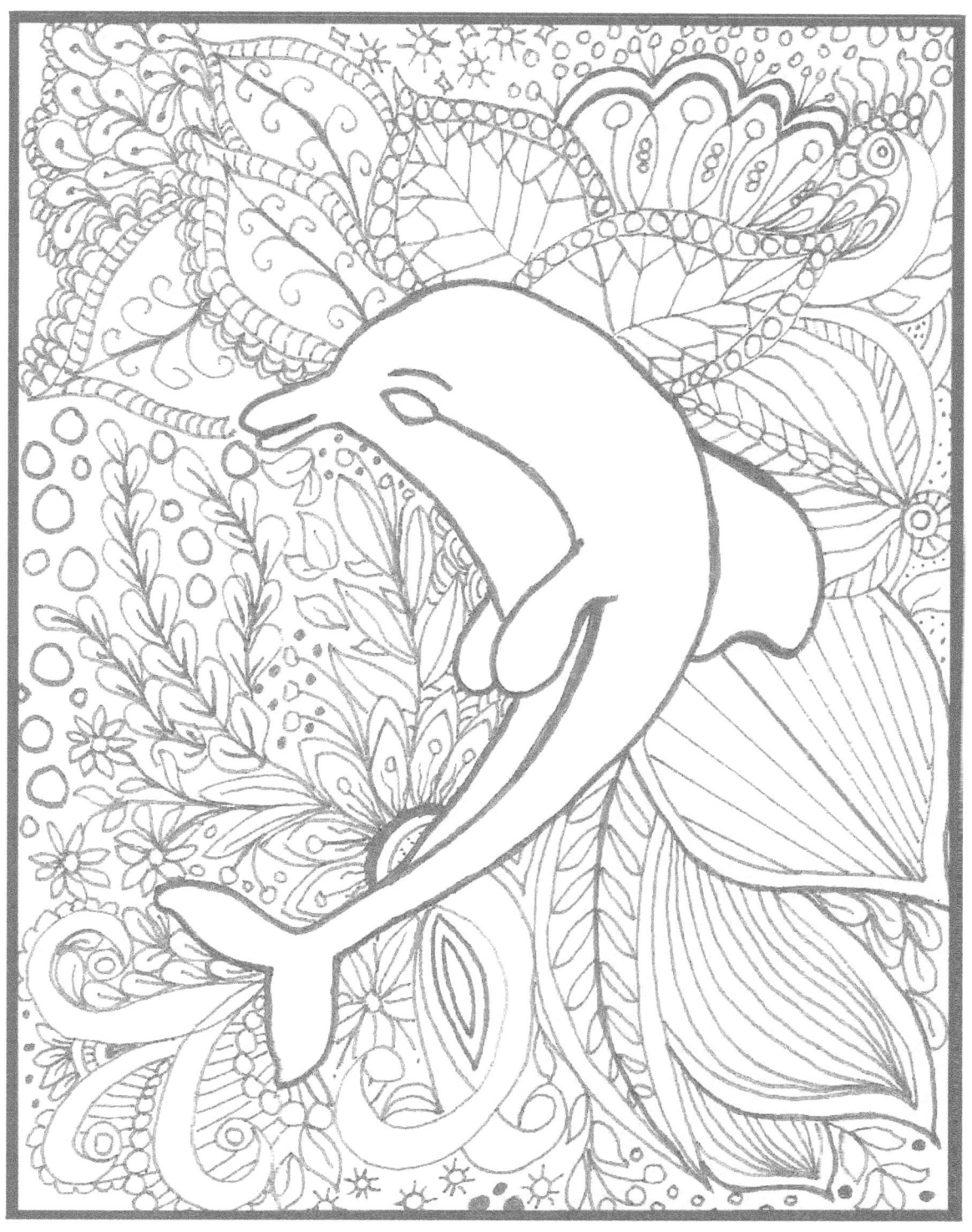

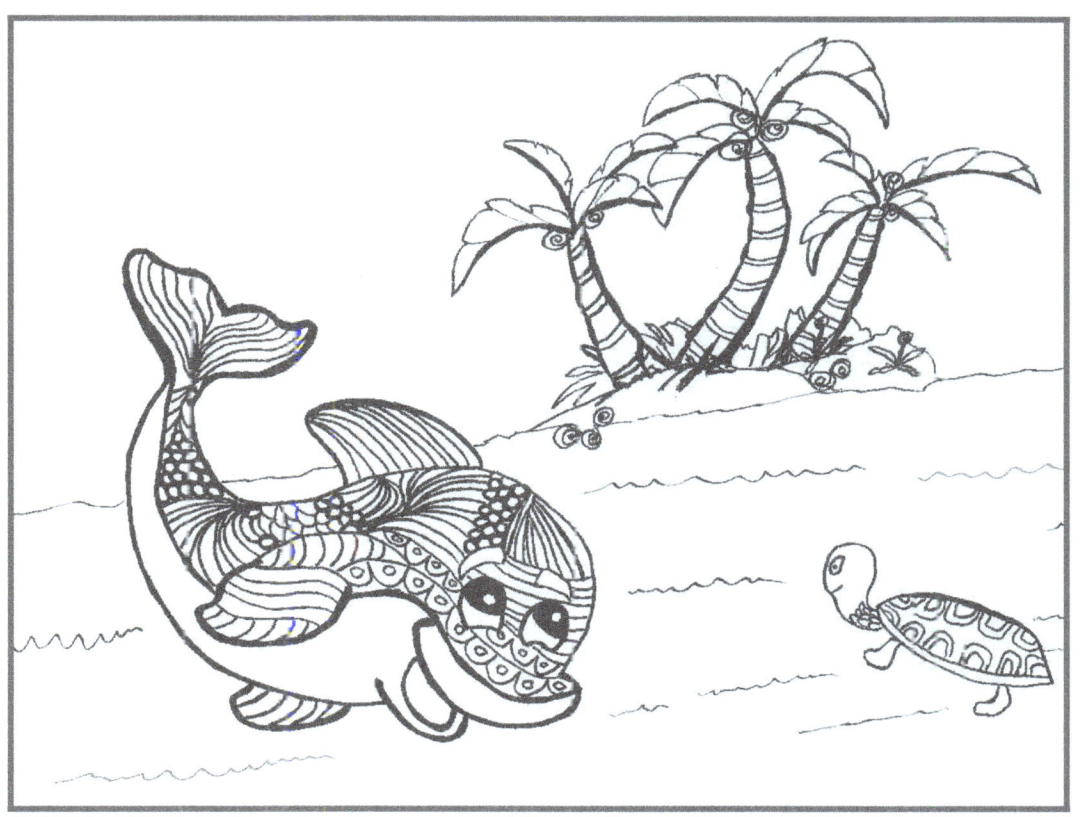

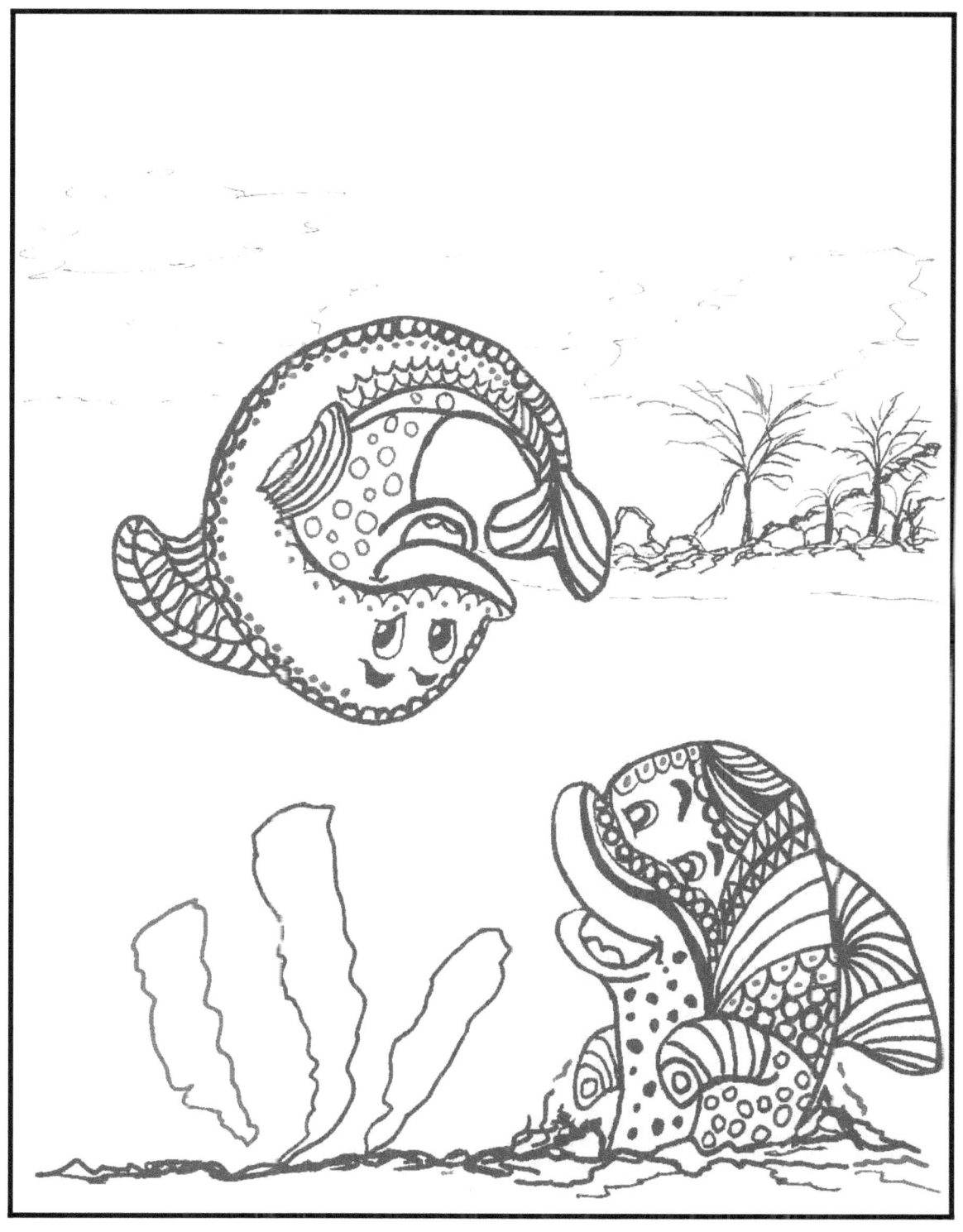

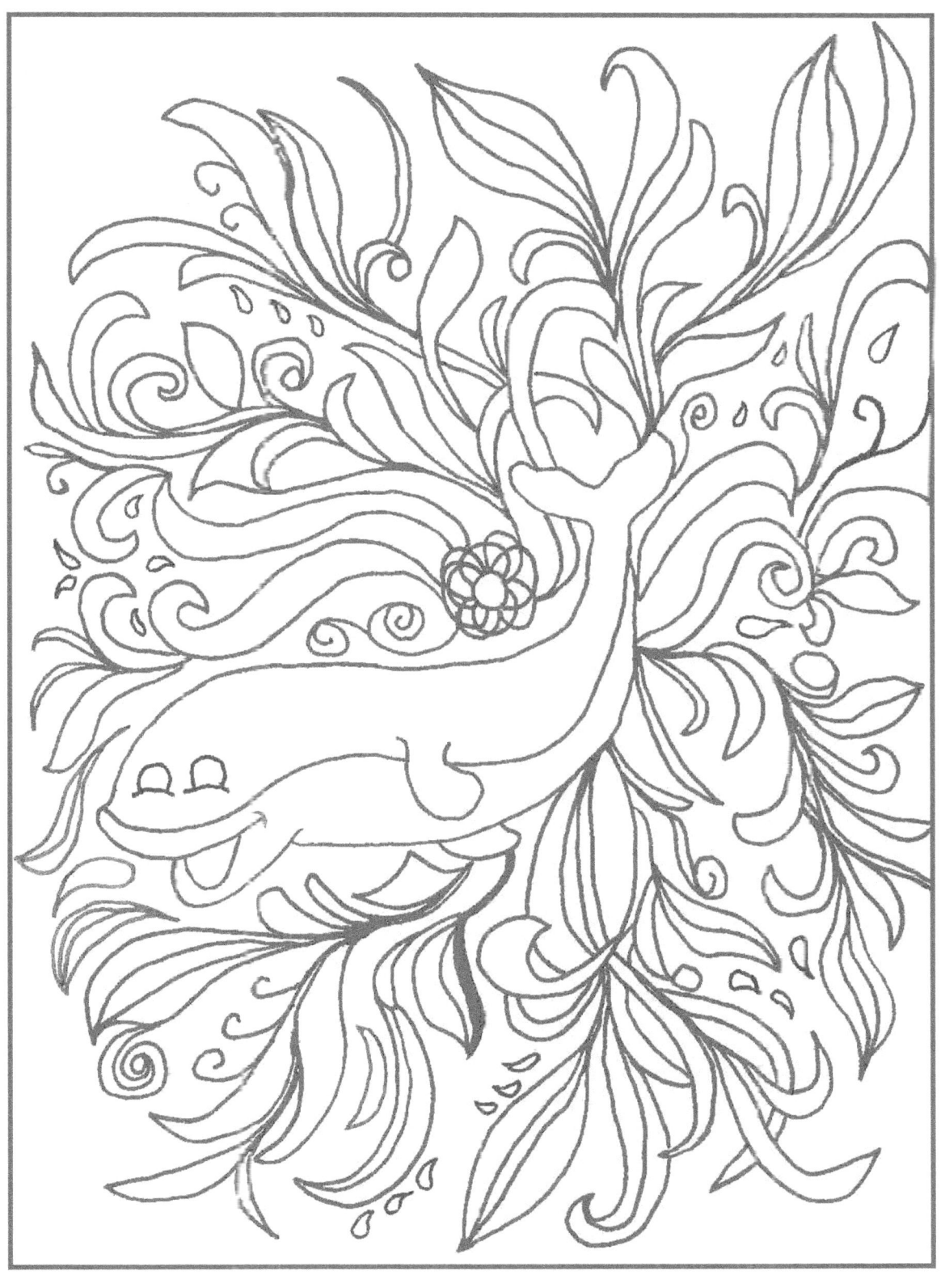

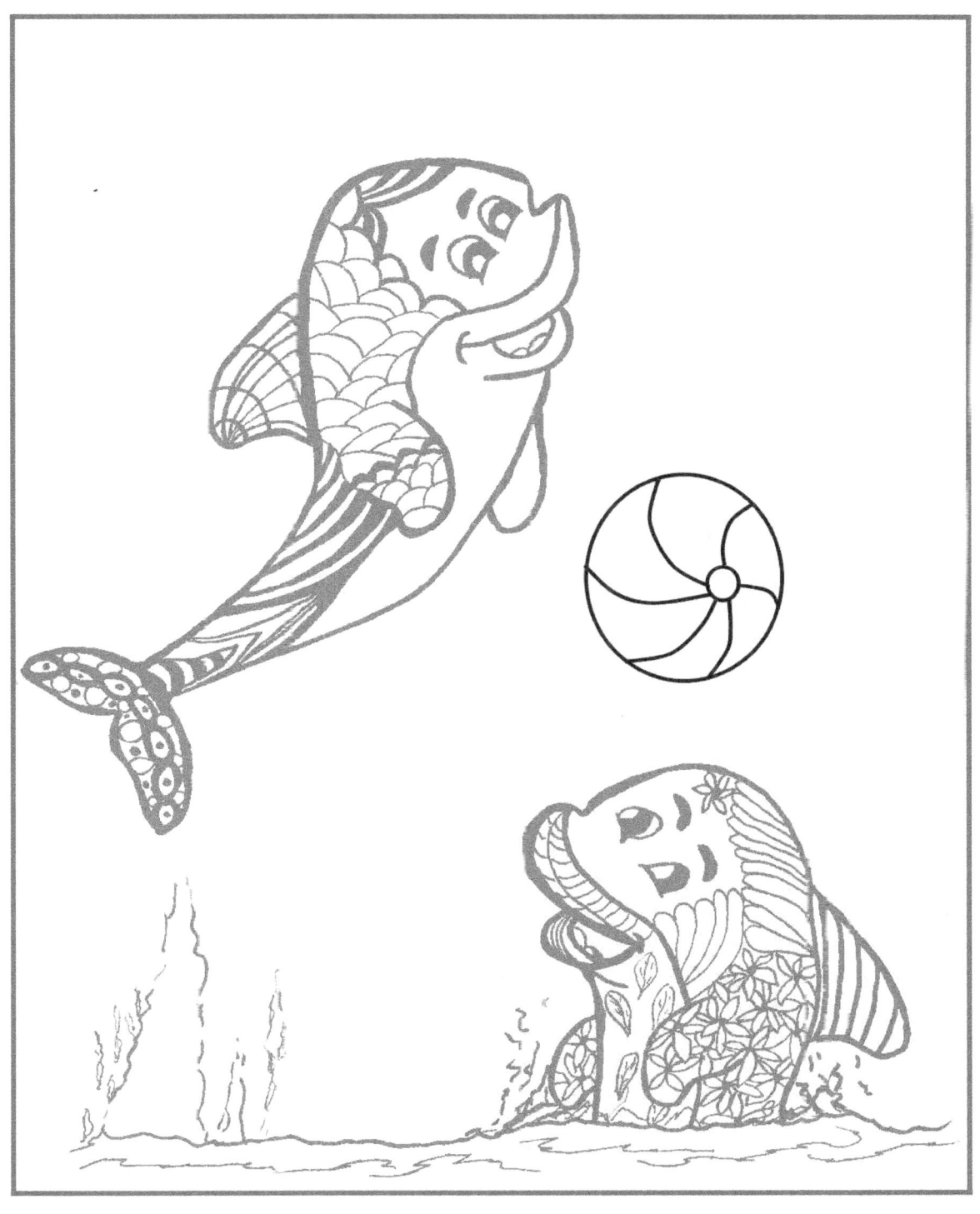

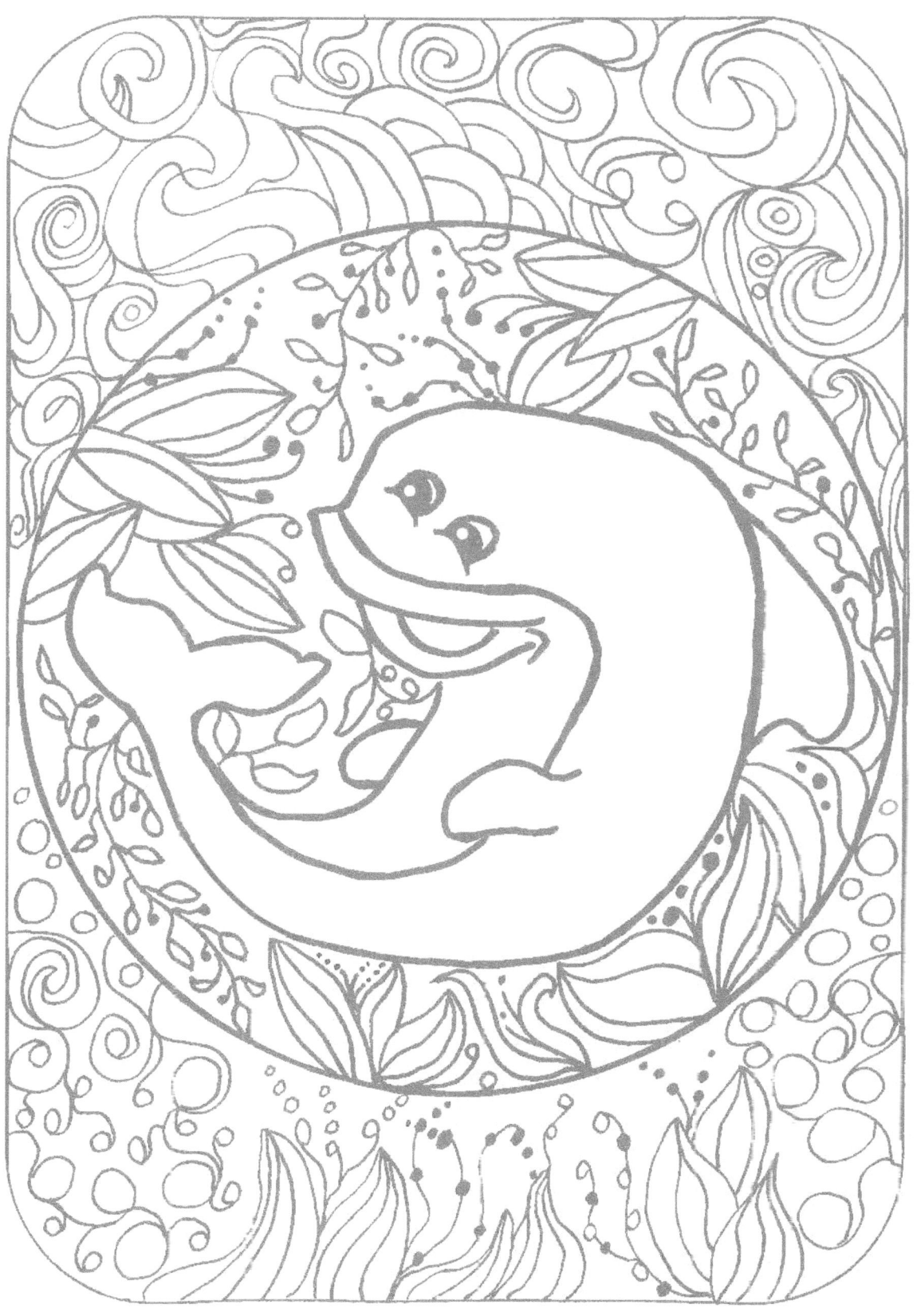

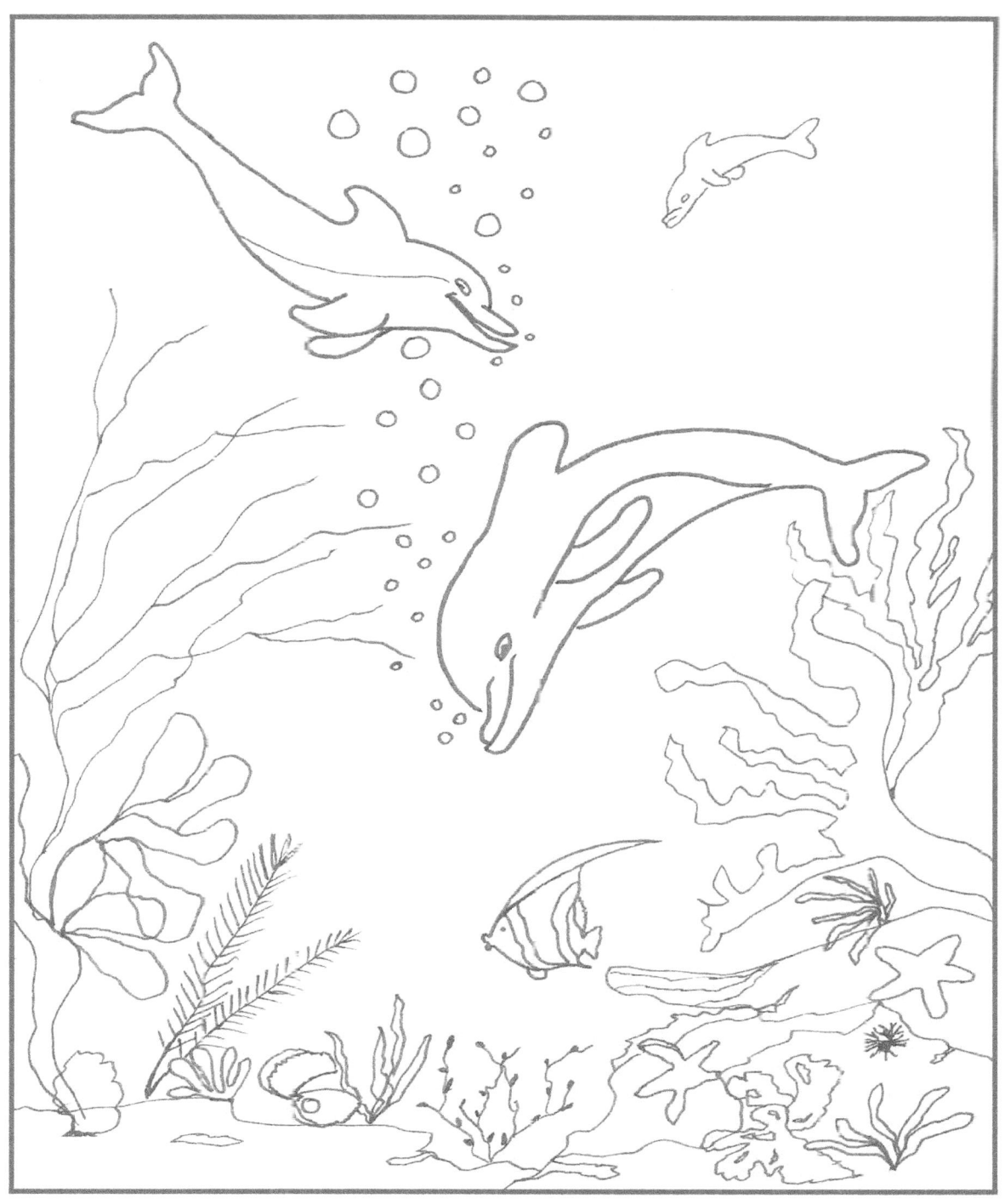

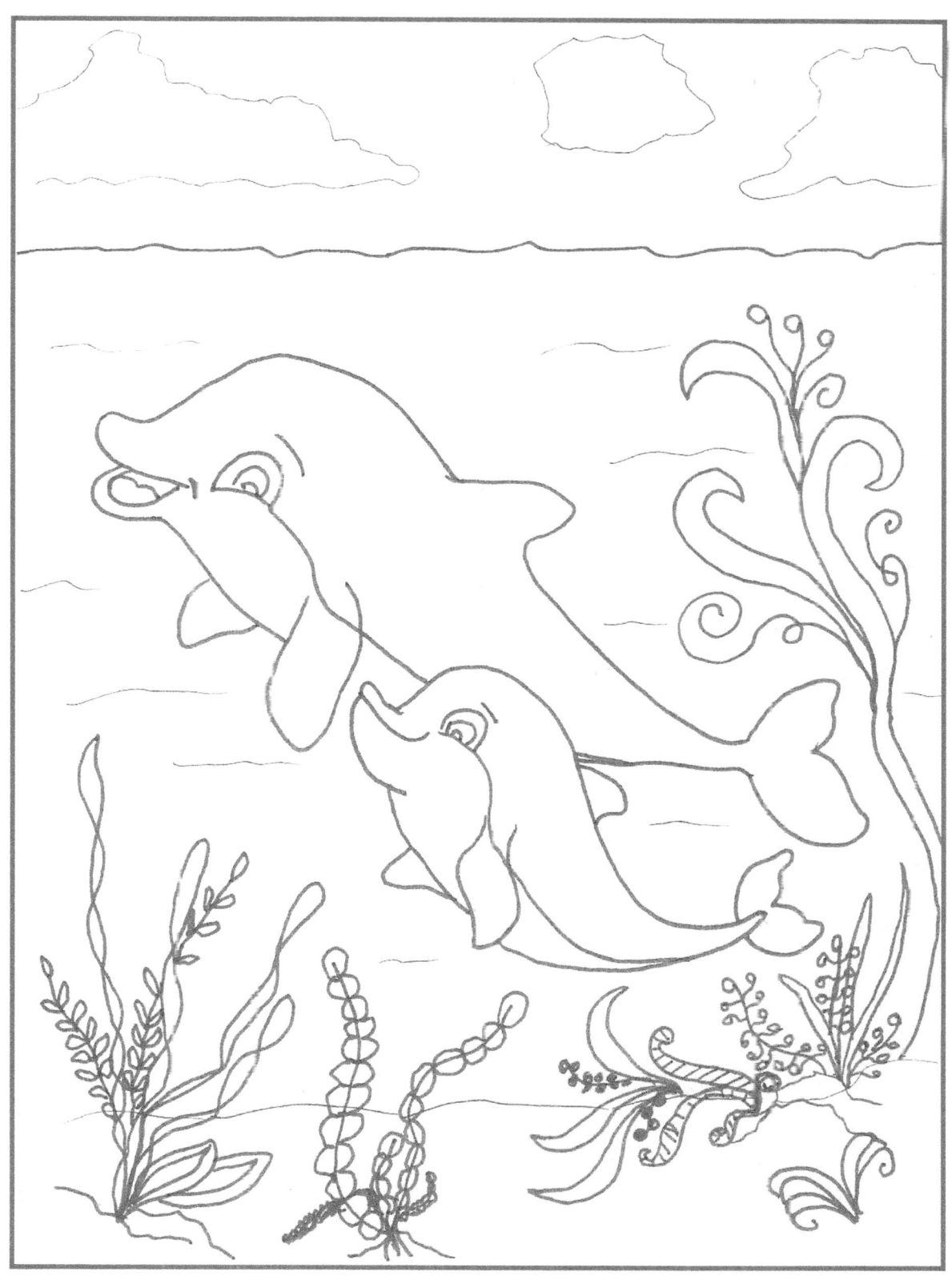

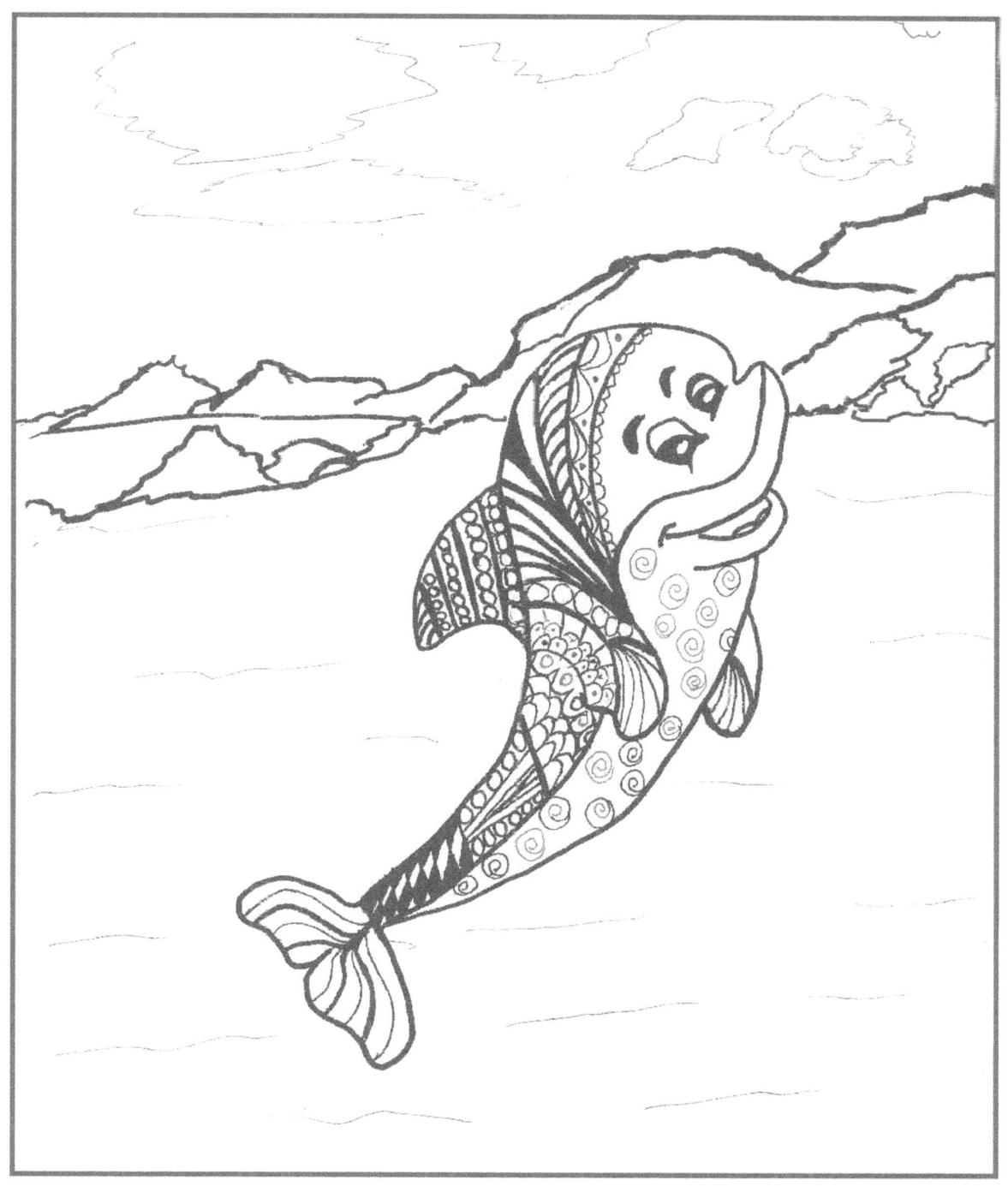

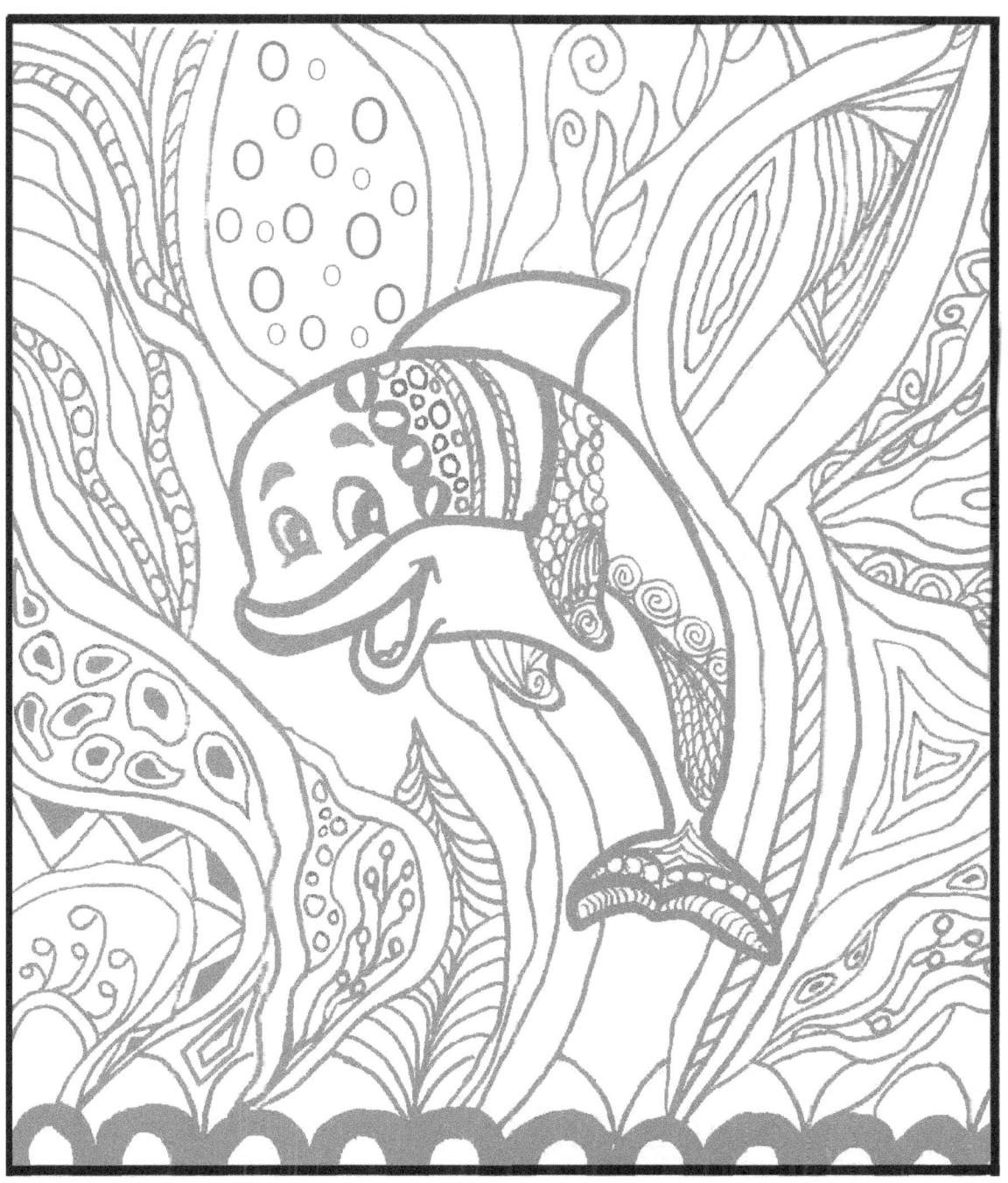

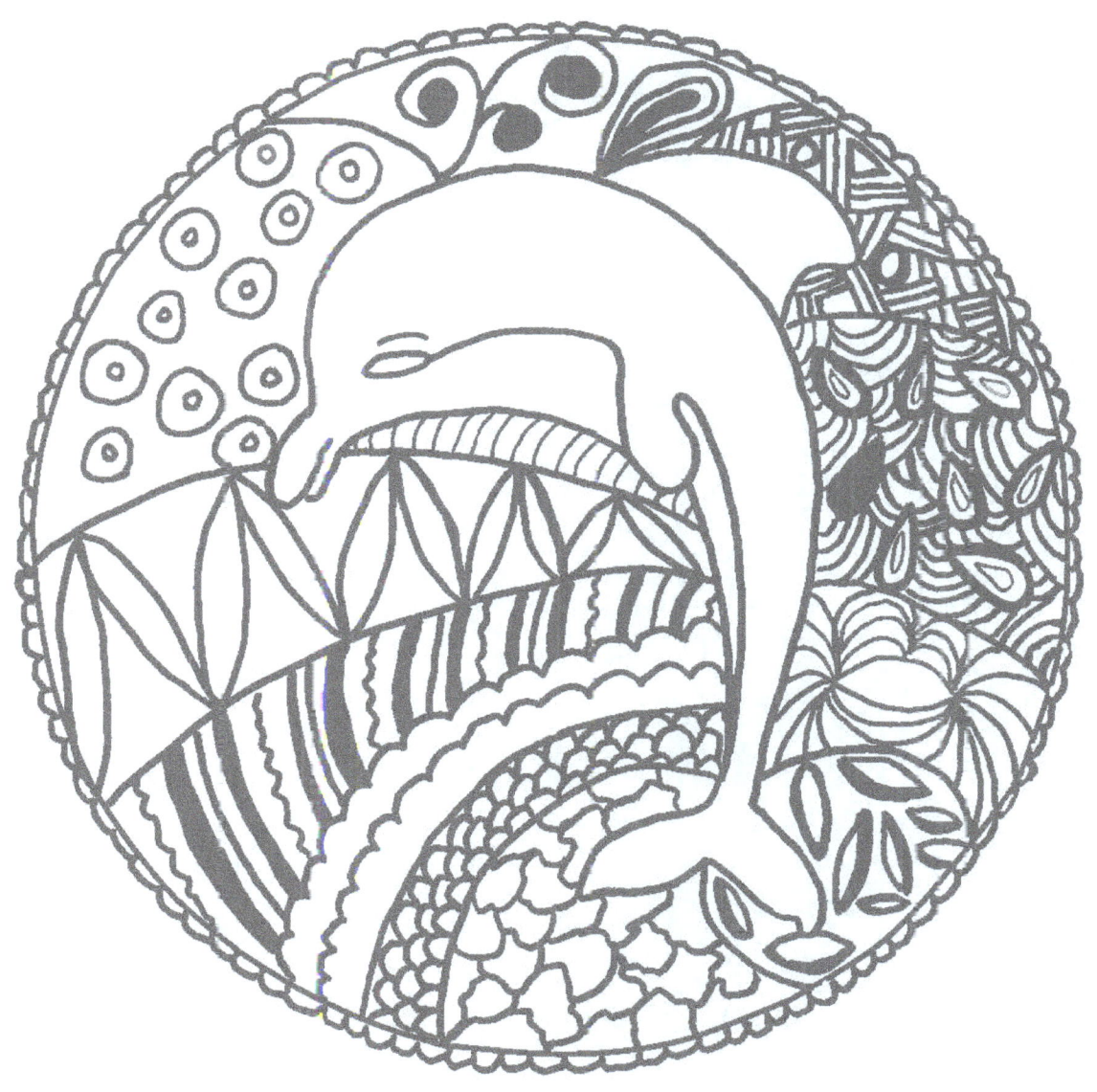

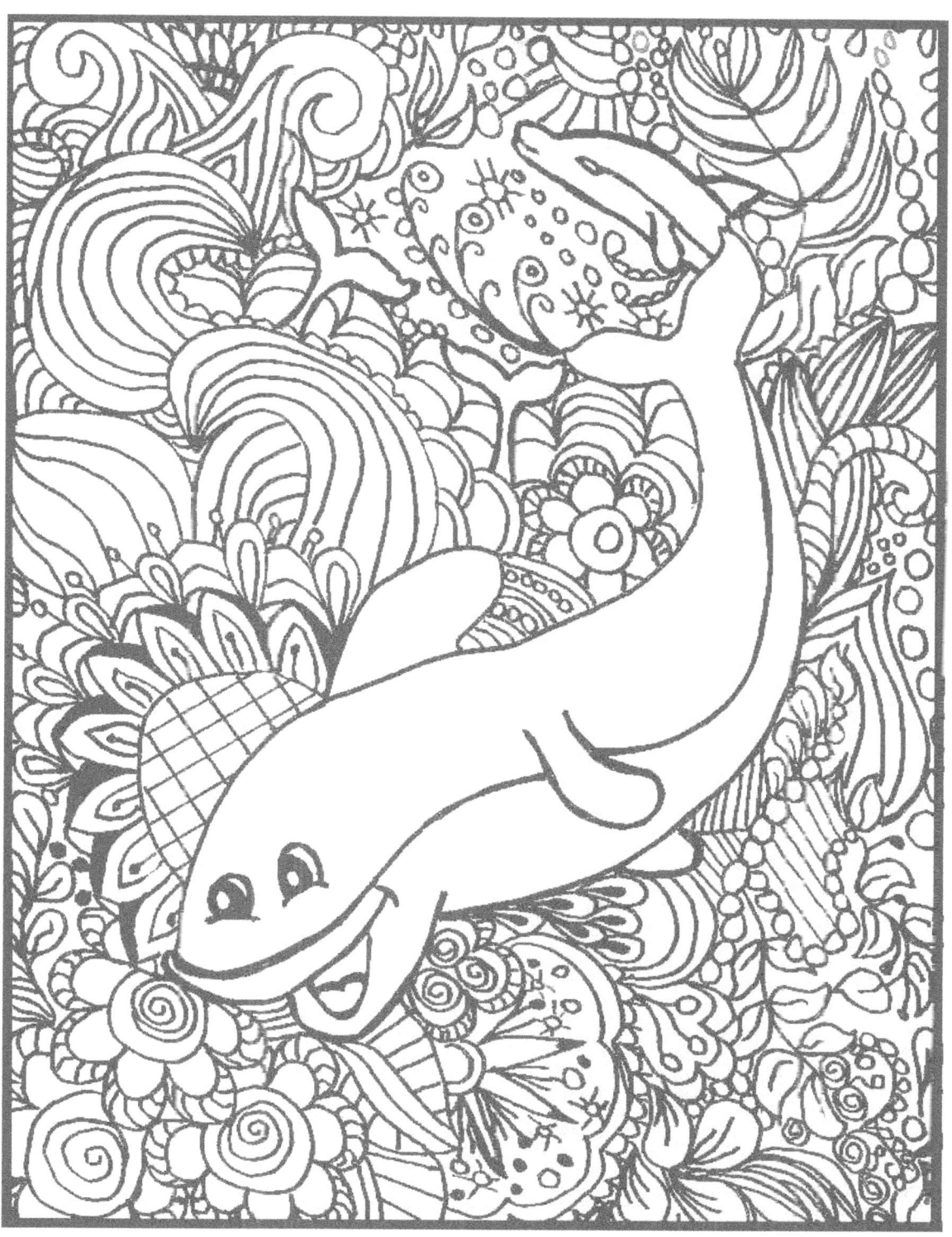

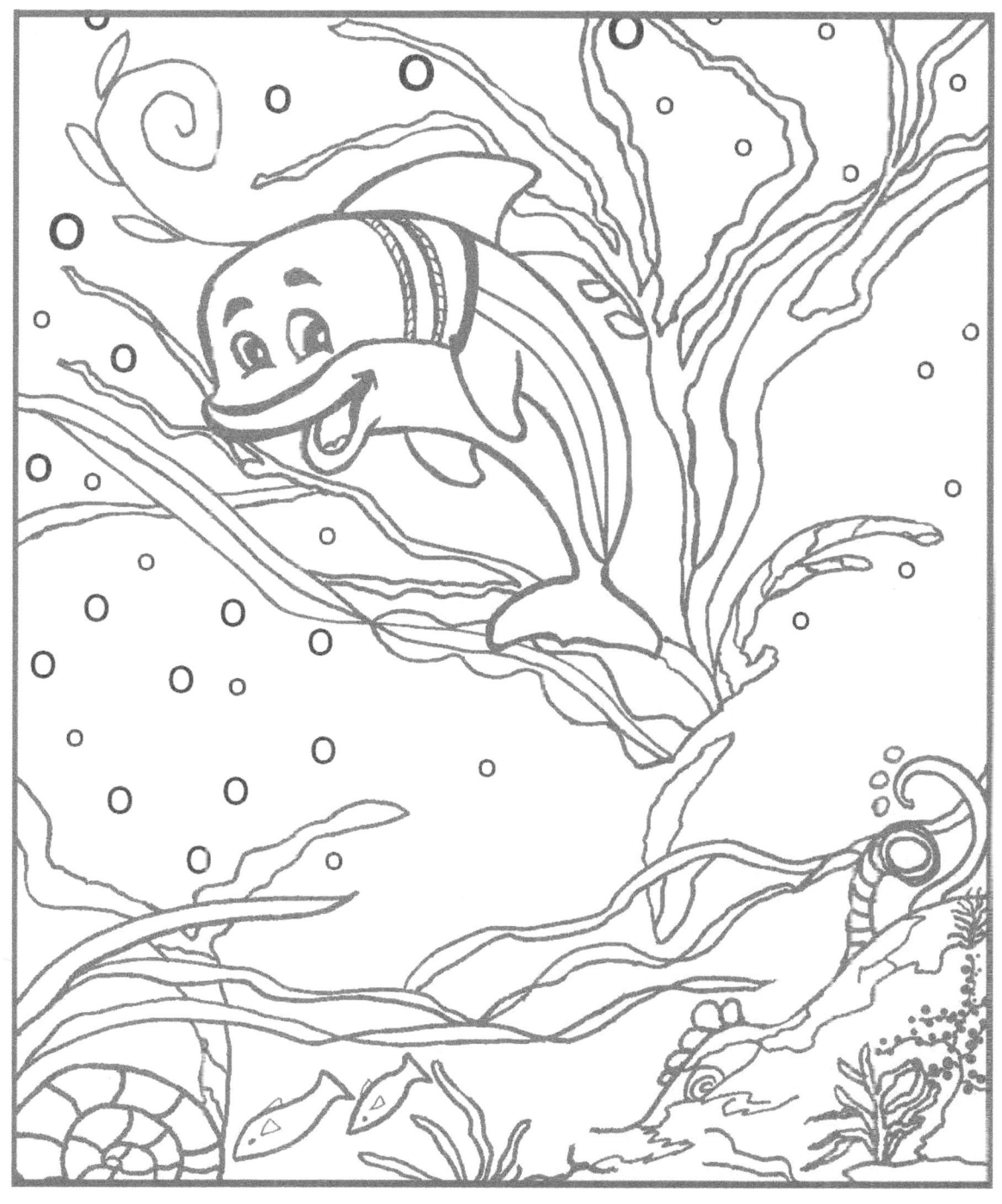

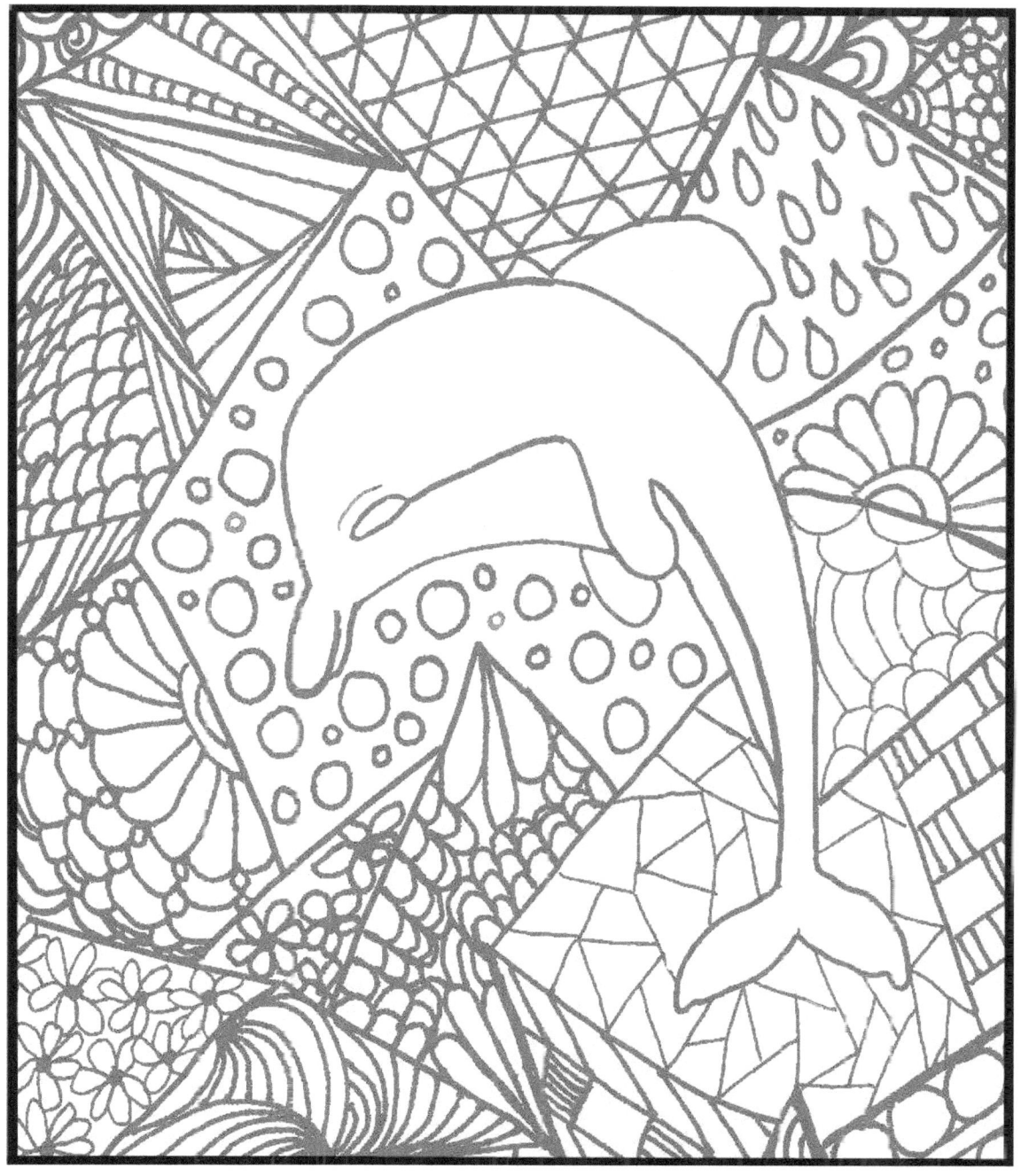

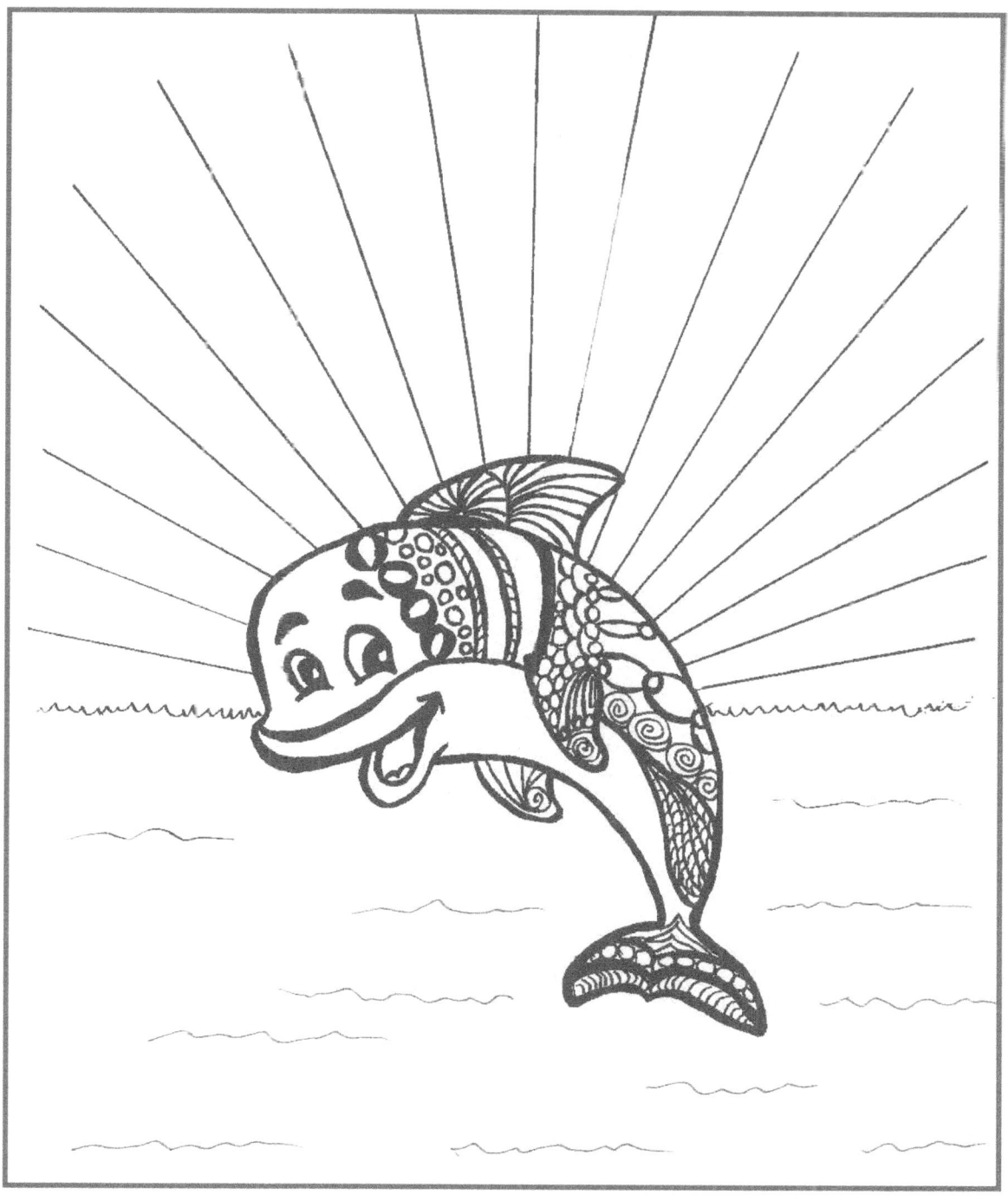

Dolphins are a favorite of mine and I hope you have enjoyed this coloring book.

More paperback coloring books can be sourced through

KD COLORING STUDIO
http://www.kdcoloring.com

Coloring and activity books for children can be purchased by searching for my author name:

Kaye Dennan

https://www.createspace.com/

www.ingramcontent.com/pod-product-compliance
Lightning Source LLC
Chambersburg PA
CBHW080542190526
45169CB00007B/2594